SILK TRAINS

by

BERNARD WEBBER

THE ROMANCE OF

CANADIAN SILK TRAINS

OR "THE SILKS"

The Word Works Publications,
1993

Copyright © Bernard G. Webber 1992

No part of this book may be reproduced or transmitted in any form by any means, electronic or mechanical, including photocopying and recording, or by any information storage or retrieval system without written permission from the author, except for brief passages quoted for review.

Canadian Cataloguing in Publication Data

  Webber, Bernard, 1914 –
    Silk Trains

    ISBN 0–9696187–1–9

  1. Silk — Canada — Transportation.   2. Railroads — Canada — Freight — History. I. Title.
HE2321.T4W42   385'.24   C93-091000-1

Cover Photo: Silk Train stopped at Jasper, Alberta. Photo 8828, published by kind permission of Canadian National Railways.

Orders & Inquiries to:	Bernard Webber
	6205 – 91st Street, R.R. 1
	Osoyoos, B.C. Canada
	V0H 1V0
	Call: (604) 495–7672

Published by The Word Works Publications
P.O. Box 1567, Station A
Kelowna, B.C. Canada
V1Y 7V8

Call: (604) 861-1587   Fax: (604) 861-5530

PRINTED IN CANADA

ACKNOWLEDGEMENTS

In undertaking the research for this book, I acknowledge gratefully the assistance given me by Connie Romani, Information Services, Canadian National Railways; by the late Omer Lavallée, former Corporate Historian and Archivist of the Canadian Pacific Railway; and by James A. Shields, Supervisor, Corporate Archives, Canadian Pacific Railway.

Nor could I have completed the research without the assistance of the National Archives of Canada and the Provincial Archives of British Columbia. Their staffs were always available for consultation and advice.

Finally, I wish to acknowledge the explanations and interpretations given to me by Ren Smuin, Penticton, retired locomotive engineer of the Kettle Valley Railway, and by my late father, Harry Webber, formerly a locomotive engineer on the Canadian National Railways out of Winnipeg.

TABLE OF CONTENTS

CHAPTER ONE — INTRODUCTION 1

CHAPTER TWO — CANADA'S FIRST LINKS WITH THE SILK TRADE   5

CHAPTER THREE — SILK CARRYING STEAMSHIPS 11

CHAPTER FOUR — SILK SHIPS AND SILK TRAINS 17

CHAPTER FIVE — SPECIAL ASPECTS OF THE SILK TRADE 25

CHAPTER SIX — SILK TREATED LIKE FRAGILE CHINA 31

CHAPTER SEVEN — A SILK TRAIN EN ROUTE 41

CHAPTER EIGHT — AGAINST THE ELEMENTS 57

CHAPTER NINE — THE LUCRATIVE TRADE	69
CHAPTER TEN — CREW CHANGE AT WINNIPEG	79
CHAPTER ELEVEN — THE SILK TRAINS WIND DOWN	83
CHAPTER TWELVE — A QUESTION OF RATES	89
CHAPTER THIRTEEN — TOO LITTLE, TOO LATE	103
APPENDIX	109

CHAPTER ONE — INTRODUCTION

For the first forty years in this century, trains raced across North America from Vancouver, Seattle, San Francisco, and sometimes from other Pacific Coast ports carrying bales of raw silk to the silk mills of New York and New Jersey. These *silk trains* as they were called — or, more colloquially, *The Silks*, — had right-of-way over all other railway traffic. Everything went to the side-track for them, even the crack passenger trains.

What caused the excitement? Was silk so important? Over the millennia, no textile has caused so much rivalry, so much hardship, so much violence and mayhem as has silk.

Mankind first learned about silk over 4500 years ago, about 2640 B.C. The Chinese had achieved the miracle of unwinding the cocoon of the silk moth. Each cocoon, not usually more than an inch and a half long, provided between 800 and 1200 yards of silk fibre. The new thread was used to weave clothes that were shimmering and beautiful. Dresses and kimonos, coats and trousers were among the garments made from silk. Although at first the Chinese had a monopoly of the means of manufacturing silk, they were willing to sell silk products to other countries. This trade created an immediate and insatiable market for silk. Moreover, all countries wanted to learn the secret of making silk so that they could develop their own industries.

Just as today when countries or companies try to keep a monopoly of their discoveries so as to command high prices for their sale, so China sought to keep the processes of making silk to itself. China succeeded in this objective for a considerable time, but the demand for silk was such that adventurers would risk their lives to steal the secret of silk production. Silk had about the same appeal as gold.

Ultimately, the secret was out and a number of Eastern and Middle East countries began to cultivate the silkworms and their prime source of food, the mulberry tree. Chinese ships carried processed silk to India and Japan among other countries. Camel and horse caravans began to carry silk, often by means of the famed *silk road,* to Persia and countries along the Mediterranean coast.

The silk road stretched across Asia from Mongolia to the Mediterranean Sea, crossing deserts and mountain passes en route. It skirted the Tien Shan mountains, but assailed the formidable ramparts of the Pamir Mountains. It passed through the romantically named city of Samarkand on its way to the easier plains of Bactria, finally reaching the Mediterranean Sea at Tyre.

If natural hazards on the way were not enough, bands of armed brigands waited for the caravans at difficult places where they thought they would have the merchants at a disadvantage. The silk road was in operation from about 125 B.C. Soon, enough silk was getting through to satisfy the demand for silk among the wealthy classes of the Mediterranean Basin and of Europe.

It is remarkable how quickly silk spread around the ancient world. Threads of silk have been found in a grave in the Upper Danube Basin associated with the Celtic Hallstat "B" civilization that flourished about 600-475 B.C. Silk was transported over the Alps into France. A piece of silk was found in a late Roman grave near Colchester, England.

In Europe, silk clothes early extended their reputation for enhancing the loveliness of women and for displaying the wealth of men. References to silk occur in Saxon poetry, and in the poetry of the Middle Ages like *Sir Gawain and the Green Knight.* At a less aristocratic level, similar references appear in *Piers Plowman,* written about 1362. Richard Hakylut in *VOYAGES AND DISCOVERIES,* published first in England about 1598 during the reign of Queen Elizabeth I, being keen to learn how the Arabians dyed their silks, urged Englishmen going to the Mediterranean littoral to write exact notes of what they learned so that if they died or were murdered, their new knowledge might get back to England.

The market for silk persisted, century after century, down to our own day. Styles in clothing would change, but regardless, fine dresses, and shirts, and bathrobes, and ties, to name only a few kinds of garments, continued to be made of silk and to command high prices.

CHAPTER TWO —
CANADA'S FIRST LINKS WITH THE SILK TRADE

Eventually Canada's turn came to participate in the silk trade. By the 1880's, much of the Eastern United States, particularly in the cities, was beginning to accumulate great wealth. Life for the leisured classes, was becoming more sophisticated. This led to a larger market for silk garments. To a lesser extent this was true for Canada also. A trade began in bringing silk from the Orient to one of the west coast ports, placing the silk into special *Silk Trains*, and sending it at the greatest possible speed for processing in the mills at cities like New York.

The Canadian Pacific Railway was not slow in capturing a share of this trade. The C.P.R. was completed across Canada in 1885. Within a year, according to J.A. Shields, Archivist and Historian for the Canadian Pacific Railway, the first cargoes of silk had been landed at the new port of Vancouver. By 1888,

560,591 pounds of raw silk had been brought to Vancouver by steamships like *Parthia* and *Abyssinia*. By 3, September, 1892, silk arrivals were a relatively common occurrence. On that date a telegram, sent by a C.P.R. official named H. Abbott to one of his superiors in the east, appeared to read as follows:

> Nine cars silk reported on Empress China stop Impossible to take this number east on passenger trains under a week stop Suggest making up special train placing one car ordinary freight between two silk cars and giving despatch stop This would however be contrary to ruling of president that only two cars silk should be placed on any train stop Please advise what we shall do in matter stop
>
> (Signed) H. Abbott
>
> *(Telegram cited by kind permission of the Corporate Archives, Canadian Pacific Railway.)*

This Telegram is reproduced on the facing page.

Mr. Abbott's suggestion of a silk train was probably the first recorded proposal that special trains be used for this purpose.

It is clear that even at this early date, senior officials of the railway were concerned about moving the silk from the Pacific to the Eastern seaboard as quickly and as safely as possible.

CANADIAN PACIFIC RAILWAY COMPANY.
TELEGRAM.

Form 167.

From Vancouver BC Sep 3 1892

Mine Car Silk reported on Empress China impossible to take this number last on passenger train inside a week suggest making up spcl train placing one car ordinary freight between two silk cars + giving despatch this would however be contrary to ruling of president that only two cars silk should be placed on any train please advise what we shall do in matter.

Abbott

Published by kind permission of Corporate Archives, **Canadian Pacific Railway**.
No. RG-2, 23144.

On 17, September, 1892, just a few days after Mr. Abbott's telegram was sent, Mr. George Olds, the General Traffic Manager of the system, wrote from his office in Montreal to "T.G. Shaughnessy, Esq., Vice-President" as follows:

> I beg to call your attention to the enclosed report from Mr. Kerr relative to the manner in which the "Empress of India's" silk cargo was handled.
>
> The circumstance of car no. 4282 catching fire was, I assume, something beyond control, and no doubt you will approve Mr. Whyte's action in holding over at Winnipeg one day, cars 57182, 25916, and 13294, but the Traffic Department finds itself very much handicapped in the obtaining and holding of this traffic against the extraordinary prompt despatch given such property at, and all the way east of, San Francisco to New York.
>
> I am informed that in the case of a large consignment ex the "Empress of Japan" the interest alone costs the consignee $80.00 per 24 hours. You will see from this how anxious consignees are always to obtain quick delivery. We obtained very little of the freight during the year ending June 1st, 1892, but we have received several large consignments since.

> The last arrivals ex the "Empress of China" were the largest we have ever received in one ship; that we obtained so much for this ship was greatly owing to the fact that the "China" on her last voyage from Yokohama to San Francisco went to her destination via Honolulu and those who intended shipping their silk by her gave us the preference with the expectation of getting their property delivered quicker. I very much fear they were disappointed.

Obviously, senior officials of the Canadian Pacific Railway, even the vice-president, wished to be informed when something interfered with the quick movement of the silk to the consignees, most of whom had their businesses in the eastern United States. Even as early as 1892, the competition from the railways out of San Francisco was very brisk.

CHAPTER THREE — SILK CARRYING STEAMSHIPS

One advantage that the Canadian Pacific had over its competitors not only in the United States, but also, when the time came, over the Canadian National Railways was that it owned the ships that carried its silks, like the *Empress of India* and the *Empress of China*. It could ensure not only that the ocean rates were right, but that the ships were in the right place at the right time to pick up the raw silk. These were the fastest ships on the Pacific. Moreover, those who operated them were able over many years to build up good business relationships with those in the Orient who were likewise engaged in the silk trade. When the Canadian National Railways began to schedule silk trains, its officials were very much aware of the advantages enjoyed by the Canadian Pacific in the trade.

Two other steamship lines on the Pacific that came to play a significant role in the silk trade were the *Blue Funnel Line* of

England, founded in 1866, and the *Nippon Yusen Kaisha (NYK)* line of Japan, founded in 1885. The Blue Funnel liners, more freighters than passenger vessels, reflected in their names the classical education of the English founders of the line. Nearly all its ships had Greek names like *Ixion, Tyndareus* and *Protesilaus* They were not fast vessels but they had the reputation of being sturdy and reliable. These were the ships used by the Canadian National Railways when that railroad entered the silk trade.

The Japanese line, which also carried raw silk to Vancouver, ultimately became the nemesis of the combined ship and rail silk trade. Eventually, it built a fleet of "specially designed fast freighters to sail direct from Japan to New York by way of the Panama Canal." That threat was not even on the horizon at the beginning of the century. The Panama Canal was not completed until 1914. The first of the new ships did not enter service until 1929, but "by 1939, they had captured 90% of the silk trade."

(W.K. Lamb, **Empress Odyssey***, page 38, in British Columbia Historical Quarterly, January, 1948.)*

We shall see later how this threat met with intense, but in the end futile, counter-measures from Canadian and American railways.

The Freight Traffic Manager of the Canadian Pacific Railway, writing from his office in Montreal to Mr. James Oborne,

Assistant to the Vice-President, demonstrated how the Canadian Pacific's silk trade had developed in a few short years. His letter was dated December 5th, 1898, and read as follows:

> Dear Sir:-
>
> The S.S. "Empress of India" which left Yokohama on the 2nd. Inst., has on board 232 tons measurement (between 6 and 7 carloads) of raw silk and silk goods. This steamer is due at Vancouver on December 14th, and I wish you would please see that the cars containing this silk are handled in one train, or are put on the Chinese special. In any event, kindly see that the silk is given the utmost despatch over our line.
>
> *(Printed by kind permission of Corporate Archives, Canadian Pacific Railway.)*

It is interesting to note that the ocean voyage was expected to take twelve days. There was, of course, no radio at this time so that when a vessel was on the high seas, it was out of contact with officials on land. On the letter quoted, someone had divided 232 tons by 35 to arrive at an answer of six with a remainder. Clearly, each box car at that time carried 35 tons of silk. Later specially built CPR steel cars seemed to carry 40 tons of silk.

CANADIAN PACIFIC RAILWAY CO.
OFFICE OF THE FREIGHT TRAFFIC MANAGER.

L.   MONTREAL, December 5th 1898.

James Oborne Esq.,
    Ass't to Vice-President.

Dear Sir:-

The S.S. "Empress of India", which left Yokohama on the 2nd inst, has on board 232 tons measurement (between 6 and 7 carloads) of raw silk and silk goods. This steamer is due at Vancouver on December 14th, and I wish you would please see that the cars containing this silk are handled in one train, or are put on the Chinese special. In any event, kindly see that the silk is given the utmost despatch over our line.

Yours truly,

Freight Traffic Manager.

We know from other sources that the raw silk was bound in bales and wrapped in heavy brown paper, criss-crossed with strong ties. In the early days, each bale weighed about 125 pounds, although in later years, 133 pounds was the usual weight of a bale.

With the new century, the silk trade increased by leaps and bounds. In 1901, the Vancouver Province reported: "August 6 last, the Royal Mail Steamship *Empress of Japan* entered port with raw silk valued at $1,000,000 and all previous records were eclipsed." Even in that newspaper story, it was reported that the *S.S. Tartar* was on its way bringing: "539 tons of raw silk valued at $1,500,000 in round figures . . ." As the "Tartar" was also bringing manufactured silk, it was estimated that the total value of the silk cargo was about $2,000,000."

(Cecelia Lamont, **The Silk Connection,** *in Canada West, Page 20)*

The report continued: "Never before in the history of the port has such a valuable consignment of silk been shipped through in transit to New York, and the fact demonstrates very clearly that the route from the Orient via Vancouver is becoming extremely popular alike with Oriental shippers and American manufacturers."

In the first decade of the twentieth century, it became clear that the elegant white Empresses, with their swept back "clipper" bows were too small and getting too old to give service much longer. Two new sister ships were laid down and launched in 1912. The new *Empress of Asia* weighed 16,909 gross tons, and the *Empress of Russia*, 16,810 gross tons. Although not the largest, they were the fastest and the most modern ships in Trans Pacific service. They were beautiful ships, soon to be resplendent in white hulls with their three buff funnels sporting the house flag of Canadian Pacific Steamships.

A Canadian Pacific Bulletin issued in 1913, under the heading ***C.P.R. Fast Run with "Silk" Special from the Orient,*** had this to say in part: "Among the large cargo brought over by the "Empress of Asia" on her first voyage was a very valuable shipment of silk for New York, which was handled by a special train of fourteen cars. Leaving Vancouver 11 p.m., Aug. 31, it arrived New York 5 p.m. Sept. 7. Seventeen days for freight, Yokohama to New York is quick work and much faster than it can be handled by any other route."

This report highlights, modestly enough, the sense of pride felt by the Canadian Pacific System in the coordination of its ships and trains to achieve this phenomenal result.

CHAPTER FOUR — SILK SHIPS AND SILK TRAINS

During the second and third decades of the Twentieth Century, the silk trade burgeoned in Canada. There was increasing emphasis on getting the new crop of silk to the processors as speedily as was consistent with safety. A C.P.R. Bulletin dated October, 1919, noted another record:

> Vancouver, B.C. - All records for silk handling were broken with the arrival from the Orient of the Canadian Pacific Steamship "Empress of Asia" on August 25. The big steamship brought in 10,000 bales of raw silk, an unprecedented shipment for a single vessel plying in the Trans Pacific trade. The raw silk cargo alone is valued at $8,500,000 and in addition, the Empress carried 2,053 cases of silk goods, bringing the value of the total silk consignment aboard easily to the record figure of $10,000,000.

$10,000,000 does not seem such a vast amount of money these days, but one has to remember that a 1919 Canadian dollar would likely have the purchasing power of fifteen or twenty dollars today. Then a Ford Model "T" cost about $560.00 new. A good pair of men's shoes cost no more that $5.00, and an ice-cream cone, usually with two scoops of ice cream and dipped in chocolate to boot only cost 5 **cents**. Even in terms of the 1919 dollar being worth $15.00 today, the value of that silk shipment would be $150,000,000. Why was there such a need for speed in getting the raw silk to market? The most frequently mentioned reason then was that silk quickly deteriorated. The Japanese later solved that problem with their fast ships through the Panama Canal. Controlled temperature probably solved the problem.

A more important reason for getting the silk to New York quickly was that the cost of insurance was charged on an hourly basis for silk in transit. Insurance could cost as much as 6% of the value of the silk shipment.

There was another reason for speed and secrecy. Silk was so valuable that those inclined might be tempted to stage a train robbery. The faster the silk moved, and the fewer train stops, the more difficult for criminals to plan a successful robbery. Also, silk trains customarily carried security guards.

If the threat of high-jacking seems far-fetched, consider the memorandum dated 30, September, 1927, from W.A. Kingsland, General Manager, Canadian National Railways,

Winnipeg, to Assistant General Manager J.R. Cameron, Vancouver, with copies to General Superintendents in Edmonton, Saskatoon, and Winnipeg. The memorandum reads as follows:

> For various reasons we have been avoiding giving any publicity to the performance of our silk trains from Vancouver, but it now appears that a travelling newspaper man from New York, who recently passed through Fort William (now Thunder Bay) secured a lot of information from one of our officers or employees and wrote quite an article about the situation, which article has been published and re-published in various papers in the States.
>
> It is not known who gave out the information, but in view of the desire that publicity of this kind should not be given, it would be appreciated if you would take up with the various officers concerned, under your jurisdiction, warning them against talking about such trains to any outsiders.

There were clearly several reasons for "highballing" the silk trains from Vancouver to New York.

To return briefly to the Trans Pacific "Empress" ships of Canadian Pacific. We have mentioned the *Empress of Russia* and the *Empress of Asia*. In May, 1914, the "Russia" steamed from Yokohama to Vancouver in the unheard of time of

8 days, 18 hours, and 31 minutes, setting a record that lasted for 9 years.

(J.A. Shields, Canadian Pacific archivist and historian interviewed in Montreal, September, 1988)

There were other "Empresses" that carried raw and manufactured silk across the Pacific for Canadian Pacific Steamships. The *Empress of Australia* was one of these. She is shown on the following pages entering Vancouver harbour when development on the North Shore had hardly begun. The "Australia" served on the Pacific during the nineteen twenties and nineteen thirties. She was bigger than the ships we have already mentioned, weighing 21,900 gross tons.

The *Empress of Canada* was launched in 1920 and weighed 21,000 tons. She wrested the record for the fastest crossing of the Pacific from the *Empress of Russia* by posting a time of 8 days, 10 hours and 9 minutes. She is shown on the following pages in the white dress that became the hallmark of the *White Empresses*.

The largest and most modern of the White Empresses was The *Empress of Japan* launched in 1929 for the Pacific service. Like the other Empresses, she carried her quota of silk. On the outbreak of the second world war, she entered war service as a troop carrier and survived the war. Unfortunately, the carrying of silk to west coast ports for trans-shipment to New York was a permanent casualty of the war.

The Empress of Asia.

Published by kind permission, ***British Columbia Archives & Records Service.***
Catalogue No. HP97359 Negative No. G6979.

The Empress of Australia.

Published by kind permission, **British Columbia Archives & Records Service.**
Catalogue No. HP97360 Negative No. G6980.

The Empress of Canada, 1920's.

Published by kind permission of Corporate Archives, ***Canadian Pacific Railway.***
Photo. No. 12936.

CHAPTER FIVE —
SPECIAL ASPECTS OF THE SILK TRADE

For information about the Trans Pacific shipment of silk, I have depended chiefly on Canadian Pacific sources. Details about the operation of silk trains will come mostly from Canadian National. The first archivist and historian of Canadian Pacific documents has written:

> Due to the fact that this office was set up only in 1973, long after early operating records were discarded, I regret to say that we possess no original references of our own to silk trains. Neither do our files contain photographs of those trains.
>
> *(The late Omer Lavallée, Retired Canadian Pacific Archivist, Historian. 13, March, 1985.)*

The present supervisor of Corporate Archives of Canadian Pacific, Mr. James A. Shields, during an interview in his office in Montreal on 31, August, 1987, said very much the same thing. On the other hand, most, if not all, of the Canadian National records about their silk trains were deposited in unsorted boxes in the National Archives, Ottawa. *(National Archives of Canada, RG30, CNR Records.)* They are an invaluable source of information about the crises, failures and successes associated with moving silk trains under time constraints across the continent.

The experiences of the Canadian Pacific with silk trains antedate those of the Canadian National by several decades. There are very few letters in the Canadian National files dated earlier than 1925. The bulk of the letters and memoranda relate to events in 1926 or 1927.

An interesting memorandum written by R.L. Burnap, Assistant General Freight Traffic Manager of the Canadian National on 18, May, 1928, is worth quoting in full because of its information about how the silk was shipped and how it was treated when it got to New York. Mr. Burnap's memorandum reads as follows:

> Raw silk is imported from Japan or China in skein form, packed in bales of about 125 lb. each. This silk in skeins is not in shape to be used either for weaving or spinning machines.

The skeins of silk are put on a winding machine. This machine winds the original raw silk thread on to little wooden spools.

These spools are transferred to twisting machines, where a number of raw silk threads are twisted together a certain number of turns per inch and made into one thread of thrown silk.

This thrown silk comes off this twisting machine on other wooden spools. The spools containing thrown silk are transferred to other machines which wind the thrown silk from the wooden spools on to proper containers; and the silk is shipped out to knitting concerns and weaving concerns in this condition.

No finishing, no dyeing, no weaving, no knitting is done. The operation of throwing can be briefly summed up as changing the form of packing the silk from the skein form to the thrown silk form.

Ninety-five percent of the users of the thrown silk were said to live and work along the Atlantic seaboard of the United States. The transformation of the skeins of raw silk into containers of thrown silk was the first operation to be performed by the importers in the east. In writing his description of the process, Mr. Burnap seemed intent on informing all Canadian

National personnel associated with the silk trade how the silk was handled when it passed beyond their ken.

What was the value of the silk? It varied widely over the years. The following anecdote conveys a graphic idea of an early comparative pricing. In 1887, the Canadian Pacific Railway extended steel from Port Moody to the new port of Vancouver. It set aside $32,000 to build a roundhouse and machine shop in Vancouver. In 1887, a car of silk weighing 30 tons was valued at between $75,000 and $95,000., or more than twice as much as both a roundhouse and a machine shop. In that year, a pound of silk was worth between $1.25 and $1.60.

*(James A. Shields, Archivist & Historian,
Canadian Pacific Corporate Archives, Montreal,
1, September, 1987.)*

The price of silk rose as time passed. On 7, May, 1929, the Interstate Commerce Commission of the United States issued a report that stated that between January, 1924, and April, 1928, the value of imported raw silk ranged from $4.20 to $8.25 a pound. Raw silk averaged $6.00 a pound in November, 1926. At that rate, a single 30 ton car of silk was valued at $360,000.

A silk train was often seven cars in length, but twelve cars were not unusual. A silk train could be valued at $2,500,000. In later years the weight of a car of silk was about 20 tons and the weight of a bale of silk had increased to 133 pounds. Silk was worth $6.00 a pound and more during the heyday of the trade before the economic depression settled in and before silk substitutes had made a negative impact upon the demand for silk.

Another set of figures gives the average price of silk in 1924 as $6.50 a pound; in 1929 as $5.11 a pound; in 1930, at $3.70 a pound; in 1934, as $1.27 a pound. Significantly, the great economic depression began in 1929 with the effect you see upon the price of silk. At $1.27 a pound, the silk trade was much less attractive than it had been.

CHAPTER SIX —
SILK TREATED LIKE FRAGILE CHINA

For their own protection, the railways had to insure each shipment of silk. The insurance companies were secretive about their rates, but they were undeniably high. We have seen that they were based on the number of hours that the silk was in transit. At the speed of the silk trains, the risk of derailment and of other accidents was great, especially in the mountains where the threat of rock slides was always present. The wonder is that there were not more accidents. Doubtless that was because from the General Manager down to the humblest track worker everyone practised the greatest vigilance. Crews went out in any weather, on speeders or on work trains, to check the condition of the tracks.

Moreover, to protect against high-jackers, armed guards usually rode each silk train. Again, for added protection, silk trains stopped only at divisional points, each 150 to 200 miles apart. They rarely stopped at public stations but in marshalling yards.

In the early days of silk transportation, box cars were used with some kind of smooth lining to protect against damage to the bales of silk. Although these box cars were given special maintenance to help them operate at passenger train speed, this make-shift adaptation was not really satisfactory. This reference is to the time when no more than two box cars of silk were officially allowed to travel attached to a passenger train.

Later, The Canadian Pacific Railway built special steel cars, with the same running gear as passenger cars. These steel cars were smoothly finished inside to minimize the abrasive action of train movement. When the Canadian National entered the silk trade, that railway used steel baggage cars, lined smoothly with wood for the same reason. Despite the protective action taken by both railways, the representatives of the importers often claimed rebates because of damages allegedly done to the bales of silk. As late as 14, November, 1931, a letter from the Silk Association of America raised the familiar complaint again:

> We are continuing to experience a great deal of trouble and considerable damage due to wooden splinters piercing the matting and shirting of silk which we receive from the Orient.
>
> ... Several checks have shown that when silk was not braced or strapped together, nearly every

instance showed damage due to splinters caused by the silk shifting in the car. However, on silk which was strapped or braced, there was absolutely no damage at all.

We believe this matter should be brought to the attention of the various carriers very forcibly, as they can surely do something to stop this trouble.

The railways did what they could to improve the situation. The Canadian National said that it wedged and braced the bales of silk to prevent damage. This procedure very likely reduced the number of bales that any one car could carry thus adversely affecting the profits from the trade.

The first letter in Canadian National Records, RG30, in the National Archives at Ottawa is dated 18, October, 1924. The last letter was written in 1941. These letters span the period of greatest activity of the Canadian National in the Silk Trade.

We have seen that the ships which brought most of the silk across the Pacific for the Canadian National were the classically named liners of the Blue Funnel Line, like the *Tyndareus* and the *Talthybius*. On the next pages are three pictures: one of a Blue Funnel ship and two of such a ship discharging bales of silk at a Vancouver dock.

Between 1, July, 1925 and 1, July, 1926 six Blue Funnel ships made fifteen trips across the Pacific bringing a total of 41,217 bales of silk. The largest cargo of 5,256 bales was aboard the *S.S. Tyndareus* when it docked in Vancouver, 9, September, 1925. The smallest cargo consisted of 1359 bales brought by the *S.S. Talthybius* on 29, April, 1926. The names of the other Blue Funnel ships bringing silk are interesting — *Achilles, Philoctates, Protesiliaus, and Ixion*. The greater frequency of Blue Funnel arrivals helped to counteract the faster times and the quicker turn around of Canadian Pacific steamships.

We have seen that silk trains varied in length. During the same year that recorded the arrival of the ships with silk for the Canadian National, four trains had five cars, four had six, four had eight cars, four had nine, and there was one each of ten, eleven, thirteen and fourteen cars. Some Japanese ships also brought silk for Canadian National. One of them was the *Paris Maru*.

In 1926, the fastest silk train to cross the continent to New York took only 83 hours, 56 minutes, which was a phenomenal time for that era. There were many transcontinental passenger trains in those great days of railways, but the fastest of these trains, *The Trans-Canada Limited* took 89 hours to travel just from Vancouver to Montreal. It then took as much as 40 hours and 56 minutes to carry the silk from Montreal to New York.

In that 89 hours, The Trans-Canada Limited traversed 2,885.7 miles for an average speed of about 31 miles an hour, including stops. The picture on page 38 shows a Canadian Pacific Trans-Canada Limited near Lake Louise, Alberta, in 1929.

The S.S. Talthybius.

Published by kind permission, **British Columbia Archives & Records Service.**
Catalogue No. HP40429, Negative No. B7022

Bales of silk loaded in slings, being transferred from ship's holds to a Vancouver dock.

*Published by kind permission of **Canadian National Railways**, Photo 3187.*

*Blue Funnel Ship discharging bales of silk at Vancouver dock.
Note how quickly the bales are moved to the waiting train.*

*Published by kind permission of **Canadian National Railways**,
Photo 12987.*

CPR Trans-Canada train near Lake Louise, Alberta, 1927.

*Published by kind permission of **National Archives of Canada**.*
Negative No. PA 49791.

It took too long for the silk trains to go to New York by way of Montreal. The fastest route was through Toronto. Although the usual daily Vancouver-Toronto Express took 90 hours and fifteen minutes, there was a linkage via Buffalo to New York that took only 14 hours and 50 minutes. By this route a passenger train could reach New York from Vancouver in 105 hours and 5 minutes. Compare this speed with that of a silk train that sometimes could travel the same distance to New York in 83 Hours and 56 minutes. That would establish a minimum difference of 21 hours, 9 minutes, or almost a full day. This was a result of high-balling the silk train all the way with few stops and those — to take on coal and water, for instance — being as short as possible.

The silk trains on the average took 90 hours and 49 minutes to cross the continent to New York. Each railway kept careful records of the elapsed time of each silk train in crossing to New York. Everyone tried to reduce the time in transit.

The scheduling of silk trains was finely tuned all the way. When a silk train was in his division, the dispatcher had to know where it was at every instant and to clear the track.

CHAPTER SEVEN — A SILK TRAIN EN ROUTE

Let us follow a shipload of silk from its arrival in Vancouver until it reached New York.

Assume that the Blue Funnel liner, *S.S. Tyndareus*, was inbound from Yokohama with 2907 bales of raw silk destined for re-shipment east over Canadian National Railways. It was due to dock first at Ogden Point in Victoria and then sail on to Vancouver. So that no time would be lost in trans-shipping the silk from ship to train, the CNR local Freight Agent in Vancouver sent a team of five workers to meet the ship in Victoria and travel with her to Vancouver. They carried the manifests for rail cars waiting at dockside in Vancouver. Their job was to make up each car manifest before the ship arrived in port. They determined which blocks of silk would go into each car. This work took them five or six hours.

This procedure, efficient for the company, was resented by the men. Wages were nothing like what they are today. There was no time-and-a-half or double-time for work beyond the normal working day, let alone for work undertaken at unusual hours or under unusual circumstances. The men were denied pay for their hours on board ship after they had finished their silk car make-up duties. At first their protests got nowhere, but eventually they were allowed straight time after freight officials in Vancouver argued their case with senior officials in Montreal.

The men also complained because there was no accommodation for them aboard ship. Finally, that were told that they might rest in the crew hospital quarters. That did not satisfy the men. They objected to sleeping in the same beds that Chinese sailors had occupied.

There were problems, too, in Vancouver. The ship's equipment unloaded the bales of silk from the holds to the dock, but who paid for moving the silk from the dock to the trains? In a letter from the Harbour Commissioner's Office to A.R. Douglas, CNR Local Freight Agent, 15, December, 1925, the Vancouver Harbour Commissioners claimed that not they but the railway should pay the 80 cents an hour per man which was then the going rate of pay.

The situation was complicated by the fact that the ships did not always dock as forecast. Fog, or storm, or any one of a number of incidents could slow the arrival of a ship. So when were the men to be asked to report for work? If asked to report at 7 o'clock but the ship did not dock until 10 o'clock, were the men to be paid for their three hours of waiting, and if so, how much and by whom? These questions would hardly arise today but in 1925 they had not been answered by negotiation and custom. Memoranda flew backwards and forwards between Canadian National officials and the Harbour Commissioners.

The issue was finally resolved in a terse memorandum dated 26, January, 1926, from W.A. Kingsland, General Manager of Canadian National Railways, West, Winnipeg. He wrote in part:

> There does not seem anything else to do but foot these bills. It is absolutely necessary in order to maintain the service in handling silk cargoes that we properly protect the situation at Vancouver.

The *Tyndareus* docked in Vancouver at 15.42K. No time was wasted. As soon as the first silk was out of the hatches, it was rushed into the first car of an eight car train that had been waiting for the ship to dock. The schedule from the docking of the ship to the loaded train leaving Vancouver follows:

Record from the arrival of
the ship to Departure of Train.

Ship docked	15.42K
Commenced discharge	16.13K
Completed discharge	17.30K
Commenced loading	16.14K
Completed loading	17.45K
Train left dock	17.52K
Arrived CN junction	18.02K

This was an amazing achievement by any standards — to unload the ship, load the eight car train, brace the silk bales so that they would not move in transit, and leave dockside, all in the elapsed time of one hour and thirty-nine minutes.

Similar records were kept for all ship to train movements. One for the S.S. Philoctetes reads as follows:

Ship docked in Vancouver	17.35K — May 10th.
First bale off	19.20K
Cars commenced loading	19.23K
Last bale off	20.52K
Cars finished loading	21.38K
Train left dock	21.48K
3370 bales	
Loading time	2 hrs. 15 min.
Average loading	2.45 seconds per bale.

If any loading/unloading pattern differed significantly from the average, railway superiors wanted to know why. One ship that had an average car loading time of 3.92 seconds per bale had to append the explanation "Long haul from seven and eight hatches delayed us."

The record of one ship was specific not only as to what happened in Vancouver but as to the duties of the crew who boarded the ship in Victoria:

S.S. TALTHYBIUS. Docked Victoria 7K April 29th. Left 8.40K. Consignments 53 - J. Skinner, J.K. Stansfeld, W.H. James, A.R. Douglas. To work at 7.30K, finished 14.20K. - 30 min. for meals. Pink manifest and check slips, loading slips (6 copies) check slips (2 copies). All marks carried out on check slips, copy bills of lading for Customs purposes each shipment, checking over ocean bills of lading and consular invoices and making up pro forma invoices for three shipments, copy checking sheet to Ballantyne (Pier) checkers, one our checker, 6 copies loading check (for) our men and Ballantyne pier men. Cargo at Vancouver. First Bale off at 16.16K last bale off 17.18K. Cars commenced loading 16.20K, cars finished loading 17.52K. Cars pulled out Ballantyne Pier 17.56K. 1359 bales . . . 4.23 seconds per bale.

Over-hiring of gangs was due to several factors. With usual cargo, because there was no such urgency as with silk, all cargo was unloaded before it was loaded into railway cars. With silk, as soon as the bales began to come off the ship, they were immediately loaded into the waiting cars. A second factor, as we have noticed earlier, arose from the fact that ships did not always dock on time. On the route from Victoria to Vancouver, fog could sometimes be very thick. Because of the number of islands between the two ports, and because of the strong tides at times, ships had to move very cautiously in fog. On one occasion, fog caused the captain of the *Achilles* to drop anchor in English Bay and not enter the port of Vancouver. As a result:

> The dock was placed at the expense of paying sixty men and six checkers a minimum of two hours on account of being called and cancelled.

(Letter to W.A. Kingsland, General Manager, CNR, Winnipeg, explaining the situation, 12, January, 1926)

The third complicating factor was that a ship often carried bales of silk for several cities of the United States like New York, Chicago, Indianapolis, Milwaukee. Cars had to be so loaded that the shipment for a given city would be readily available and not at the end of the car when the train stopped at the city. The necessary bales of silk had to be loaded near the doorway of the car. All this took extra time and careful planning.

Top officials in Winnipeg, the western headquarters of the Canadian National Railways, far from the action, were inclined to be critical of what the officials on the spot were doing. On 27, January, 1927, the Assistant General Manager in Winnipeg wrote L.F. Muncey, Superintendent of Transportation, Vancouver, as follows:

Silk Traffic

I observe that for the past three silk shipments there has been a gradual increase in the average time consumed in loading per car at the dock, as disclosed by the following:

> Dec. 22 .... 11.2 Mins.
> Jan. 13 .... 19.1 Mins.
> Jan. 25 .... 21.0 Mins.

Prior to the period above-mentioned I note the average time occupied in loading per car rose from a low of fourteen minutes for the shipment September 23rd to twenty-seven minutes for that of November 23rd. Kindly let me have particulars of the circumstances which result in the fluctuation.

What is Mr. Muncey to do when he gets this memorandum? He did what all officials do in a circumstance of this kind. He asked the official next below himself in the chain of command. Accordingly, Mr. Muncey asked the Local Freight Agent for the answer to the question. The Local Freight Agent replied in a memorandum dated 27, January, 1927.

He argued that it was more accurate to determine speed of loading on a per bale rather than a per car basis. The number of bales loaded into a car fluctuated considerably, governed, in part, by the destination of the various quantities of silk.

In a particular case, the freight agent explained that so far as the *S.S. Talthybius* on 13, January, 1927, was concerned " . . . our average for loading was much longer on account of silk goods for New York consisting of 80 cases all coming out of hatch #3, and not being unloaded until the very last . . . ." Again we have a glimpse behind the scenes. In this instance, the situation was beyond the control of the men on the spot. The explanation continued:

> Our competitors also had two cars loading ex the above steamer their two cars finished at 16:20 or 7 minutes before our cars finished. In addition, we had very inclement weather to contend with ex the above steamer, it snowing heavily all the time this cargo was discharging.

Was there some chagrin because Canadian Pacific, which commonly used its own steamships, got its silk off first? Finally, the Freight Agent admitted: "Sometimes we seem to have gangs that put very much more vim into their work than others."

Certainly, all officials were edgy about the handling of the silk trade. One disadvantage that the Canadian National usually had to overcome was that it normally used slower ships than did its competitors. That meant that time had to be made up elsewhere if the Canadian National was to remain competitive. Yet speed had to be tempered with caution. On 13, November, 1926, J.R. Cameron, Assistant General Manager, CNR, Vancouver, complained that ". . . some of the silk trains are moving at excessive speed between the dock and our yards . . . ." From the men's point of view, it must have seemed a case of being damned if you do or damned if you don't. At times, the condition of the road bed dictated slow speed. On 17, February, 1926, a speed limit of 35 mph was placed on traffic between certain mileages. Worse, the speed limit at that time between certain other mileages was only 15 mph.

Besides the question of deliberate speed, and that of hiring the loading and unloading gangs according to the availability of work, there were other problems that bedeviled smooth movement of the operation. One was getting enough silk cars to ship-side in Vancouver in plenty of time to ready the cars to carry silk. This complaint was made from a Vancouver official to A. Wilcox, General Superintendent of Transportation, CNR, Winnipeg, in a memorandum dated 23, August, 1927. He complained that he had needed fourteen cars for a train on 15, August, 1927, but they came two or three at a time over several days. When the ship was going to dock twenty-four hours ahead of schedule, cars had to be rushed from the east to make up the necessary fourteen.

Only four of the cars received had been in silk service previously. Men had to work until 7 o'clock in the evening on the Saturday, and again on the Sunday morning to line the inside of the cars to receive silk. This cost an extra $194.79 — not a large amount today, but a very healthy extra charge in 1927. Vancouver finally urged Winnipeg not only to return silk cars to Vancouver well before the expected arrival of a ship, but, so far as possible, to return only cars that had previously carried silk. We know that cars that carried silk had to be padded against the raw silk bales being damaged.

An interesting sequel occurred to this exchange. On 9, September, 1927, Winnipeg complained to Vancouver saying that ". . . there must have been some negligence on the part of the Car Department at Vancouver in preparing equipment for the last silk train due to the fact that one hot box developed on car 8676." The Vancouver official replied 13, September, reminding the Winnipegger that he had requested an early delivery of silk cars to Vancouver. He justified the work of his men saying:

> All concerned fully appreciate the importance of careful examination of journals, brasses, wedges, and the packing of journal boxes of baggage cars assigned to silk service and having discussed this matter with Car Foreman Hickenbotham, who personally supervised the preparation of the 21 cars for the two silk trains which left here 8th; he assures me that all journals and brasses on these cars were carefully examined and all boxes redoped and Supt. of Transportation advises that

both these trains arrived New York within 91 hours.

Our train left the Vancouver dock at 17.52K, moving slowly over the points of the switches, restrained only by the speed limitations existing within the Vancouver yard. Moving smoothly, the train soon crossed the Fraser River bridge near New Westminster and proceeded up the Fraser Valley. High mountains lay to the west and east of the mainline, with the noble volcanic cone of Mount Baker soon visible to the North-East. By this time, the train was moving at full thrust, approaching the river gorges beyond Hope, carefully rounding the innumerable curves as it moved into the mountains.

We know that the emphasis was always upon the maximum safe speed for the silk trains. That order placed enginemen and conductors in a quandary. What was that speed? Should one race through the Fraser River lowlands in the certain knowledge that those speeds could not be maintained in the mountains? Engineers had to use their own judgement, but were sometimes criticised by edgy superiors who thought that here or there they either moved too fast or too slowly. There are said to have been cases where silk trains covered 100 miles in 100 minutes. That, if true, had to be on the level prairies where the rails ran straight for miles. Such speeds were simply out of the question in the mountain divisions of both railways.

Careful records were always kept of the elapsed time required by each silk train to pass through a division or subdivision. The exact time that one train took to traverse the Yale subdivision of the Canadian National Railways is recorded below. In the following quotation, Meehan is the engineer and Baillie is the fireman:

Running Time over District:

Yale Subdivision

Eng. 5115, Meehan and Baillie, ordered 17.15K, Feb. 17.

C.N. Jct. (Leave) 18.05K
Port Mann (Leave) 18.47K
Boston Bar (Arrive) 22.03K
ELAPSED TIME YALE SUBDIVISION .... 3' 58"
(32.9 Mph)

If you have seen the railway below you as you drive through Boston Bar on the highway, you will understand why the train travelled over this subdivision at only 32.9 mph.

The mountains of British Columbia presented, and continue to present, enormous problems for the building and operation of railways. On the following pages are three pictures printed by kind permission of the National Archives of Canada at Ottawa. The most hair-raising picture is that of a freight train stopped at *The Jaws of Death,* high above the gorge of the

Thompson River on a winding track, where rock falls are a constant hazard except in winter when snow slides become the hazard. This is an old picture of track that may now be abandoned, but it is representative of much of the terrain through which the tracks still pass. The picture seems to antedate installation of air brakes applied from the engine because three brakemen are standing on the "running boards" centred on top of each box car. The brakeman nearest the caboose holds the wheel on top of the end of the box car. By turning the wheel, the brakeman manually applies the brakes to the box car. The brakemen had to move along the top of the train applying the brakes as needed to each box car in turn. That is why a brakeman was originally called a *brakeman*. Another member of the crew leans against the telephone pole near the rock cut. Beside him stands the conductor in charge of the train.

The second picture shows the CPR track alongside Kicking Horse Canyon in the Rockies. It does not take much imagination to see how easily a derailment could occur if the train ran into a fall of rock.

The third picture about the construction of a snowshed on the Canadian Pacific dates from the turn of this century, but the type has not changed much. Despite the enormous strength built into snowsheds, they have been known to collapse under the sudden weight of an avalanche of snow and debris. Such a collapse can imperil any train and the men aboard.

"Jaws of Death", Thompson Canyon. CPR — B.C.
Published by kind permission of **National Archives of Canada**.
Negative No. C7676.

Lower Kicking Horse Canyon, CPR — B.C.
*Published by kind permission of **National Archives of Canada.***
Negative No. C7672.

CPR — Construction of Snowshed.
Published by kind permission of **National Archives of Canada**.
Negative No. C7674.

CHAPTER EIGHT — AGAINST THE ELEMENTS

The railways took so much care to smooth the path of the silk trains that accidents and misadventures were rare. A railway liked to report, as the Canadian National did on 5, January, 1931, that a silk train with five cars of raw silk ex the *S.S. Arabia,* running a tight schedule from Vancouver to Jasper was still seven minutes ahead of the schedule in arriving at Jasper, despite a scheduled time allowance of not quite seventeen hours — a remarkably outstanding achievement for that day. Ten days later, on 15, January, 1931, it was reported that a seven car train ex *S.S. Teucer* was seven minutes ahead of schedule in reaching Jasper with a heavier train and a time allotment four minutes shorter than for the train carrying silk from the "Arabia". It was by such short margins that records were made.

Engineers often got their orders written on tissue-like pieces of paper called *flimsies*. The engineer usually picked up his first order at the dispatcher's office before starting his run. If orders had to be changed or amplified, the changes were tapped out in morse code by telegraphers to smaller stations on the route of the train. If the train was not due to stop at such a station, someone, a telegrapher or the station master, would type out the message on a flimsy, put it on a spiked stick and have one of the enginemen snatch it off as the train slowed through the station.

One flimsy, issued on 4 February, 1931, read:

> eng.5039 run silk extra leaving Port Mann on Wednesday, Feb 4th, as follows, with rights over all trains. Lv. Port Mann 10.00. Arrive Boston Bar 13.28.

Something must have gone wrong on this occasion. A second flimsy in due course noted that the train was two hours late. This was followed by a third flimsy that said the train was now 2 hours and 25 minutes late.

Let us suppose, however, that our train moved on time. Its movements were logged at a number of divisional and subdivisional points clear across the country, at places like Boston Bar, Kamloops Junction, Albreda, Red Pass, Jasper, Calder, Biggar, Rivers, Winnipeg, Armstrong, Nakina, Hornepayne, Foleyet, Capreol, South Perry, Todmorden,

Toronto, Bridgeburg,, Black Rock. Soon afterwards, the train passed into the United States on the D.L. & W. Line, proceeded to East Buffalo, and finally, to New York City. On this run, the elapsed time from Vancouver to New York City was 90 hours and 52 minutes, or three days, eighteen hours, and fifty-two minutes, well over a day faster than the fastest passenger train of the day covered an equivalent distance. The train must have travelled flat out across the prairies. It is unlikely that very fast speeds were possible east of Winnipeg through the Canadian Shield part of Ontario where the track curves constantly. Not all silk trains were as fortunate as the one we have just accompanied. On 23, December, 1926, a derailment was reported in the Ashcroft subdivision near Kamloops.

On 25, March presumably in 1925 or 1926, J.H. McKinnon sent a telegram to all concerned that read as follows:

> At 22.50K train 403 (not the silk special) reports striking large boulder mileage 32 - 5 Clearwater sub breaking guide yoke and disabling motion on right side eng 2510. Sectionman from McMurphy using dynamite cleared rock at 150K, eng 5110 from Blue River arrived at slide at 145K pulled No. 403s train back to Wire Cache to clear silk special and will handle 403s train to Kamloops Jct. Eng 2510 returning to Blue River for repairs, delays to traffic silk special one hour fifty four minutes No. 403 five hours, No. 404, one hour thirty mins.

Is the CNR Train Really Racing a CPR Train Across the Prairies?

*Published by kind permission of **National Archives of Canada**.*
Photo No. PA 37487.

On 18, October, 1926, L.F. Muncey, Superintendent of Transportation, CNR, Vancouver, wired J.R. Cameron, Assistant General Manager, Winnipeg, as follows:

> Running time for silk train Kam.Div. seventeen hrs. thirty-two mins. being one hr. twenty-two mins. behind schedule delayed as follows Yale Sub fifty-five mins. account slide mileage six point four STOP Clearwater Sub. Twenty-three mins accounts careful running due heavy wind and rainstorm STOP Albreda 4 mins same cause STOP For thirty-six hrs. previous we experienced very heavy wind and rainstorm from Avola East also Lytton West and intermittent rains with heavy winds between Avola and Lytton STOP Was threatened with washout at mileage eight point five Clearwater Sub. which was protected with ditches at that point STOP All creeks on Clearwater and Albreda subs. running full of water STOP

Mr. Muncey's laconic telegram to Mr. Cameron veils the high drama of this occasion. Imagine section gangs, clad in rain gear streaming with water, working with super-human effort to keep the creeks and ditches running free so that washouts will not occur.

These telegrams graphically demonstrate that railway operation is far from uneventful. We glimpse the resourcefulness of men and officials in emergencies. The sheer grit of railroaders is in a curious way almost a guarantee that the train will get through. It is unlikely that these hazards of railroading have changed much since the passing of the age of steam.

Notice the characteristic diction of railroaders in their reports. This and their parsimony with words are partly due to the nature of telegrams, now almost a thing of the past. It was and is characteristic of railroaders that they keep to basic essentials. The descriptions are apt and colourful. Both Mr. McKinnon and Mr. Muncey would be surprised if they were accused of writing literature, but they write vividly so that one sees and feels the situations that confronted them.

Railway accidents happen and silk trains were not immune from them. There is an interesting implication in a telegram from Mr. Muncey to Mr. Cameron on 14, April, 1927. It read:

> Silk train running two hours late out of Blue River, being delayed by derailment Mile 18 Clearwater sub stop Governor-General's equipment left Vancouver 9.29K stop Other trains on time stop. Everything O.K.

Note that the emphasis is upon moving the silk and only secondarily concerned with the Governor-General's train.

Usually, senior officials of the Canadian National Railways accepted explanations for a silk train's falling behind schedule.

It was a different matter if a reasonable explanation was not forthcoming. Then an official might get a telegram like the one from N.B. Walton in Winnipeg to B.T. Chappell in Vancouver.

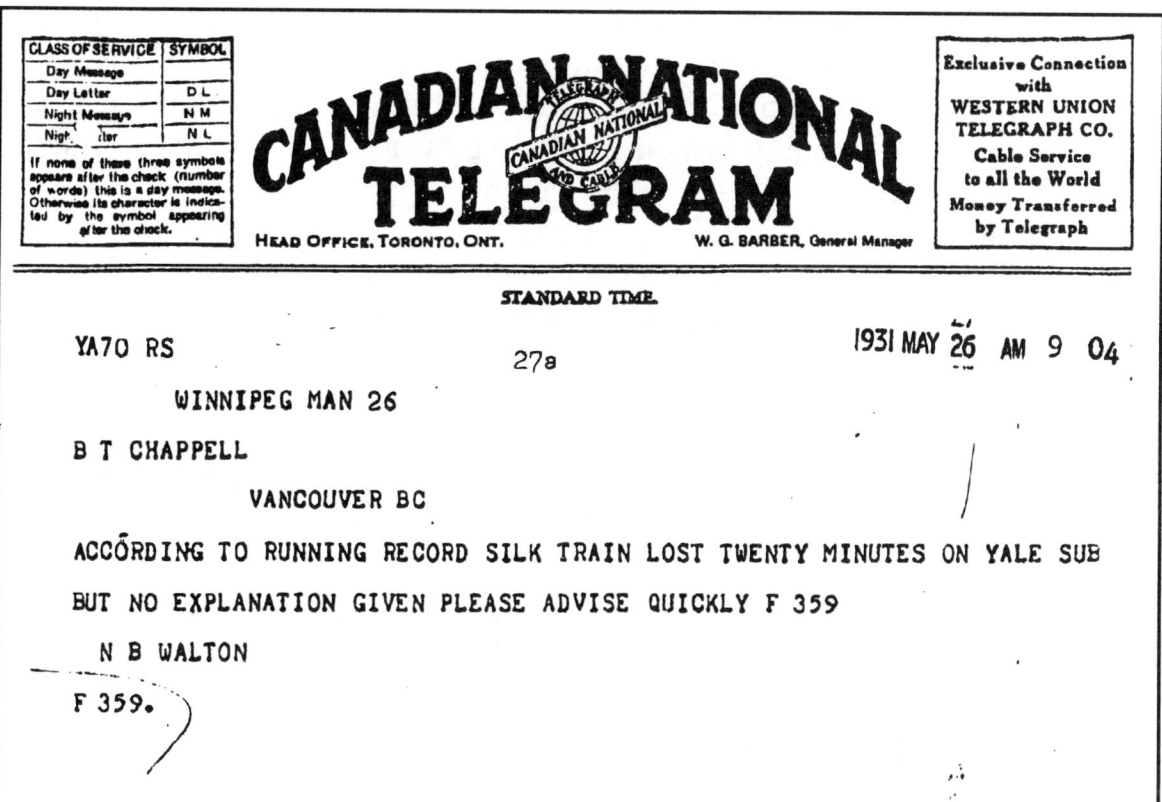

Published by kind permission of *National Archives of Canada*.
RG30, CNR Records.

Senior officials continued to exhort their subordinates to overcome difficulties like heavy weather. D. Crombie, Chief of Transportation, CNR, from head office in Montreal, wrote to A. Wilcox, General Superintendent of Transportation in Winnipeg on 6, July, 1927. In his letter he argues that although heavy rains were given as the cause of the delay of a silk train, it was now summer and he could not think that rain could cause such "track conditions" as "would warrant loss of time on the summer schedule." He went on:

> In any case we must be mindful of the fact that we are obtaining this silk traffic in competition with faster boats on the Pacific, and in competition with the Great Northern and Canadian Pacific, who apparently find no difficulty in maintaining the schedules, and I must ask that these schedules be maintained.

Although the tone of the letter is conciliatory, it leaves no doubt about its intent.

A constant theme throughout the years of the silk trains was the search for a compromise between safety and speed, with no one being satisfied. On 12, July,1927, a Vancouver official wrote Mr. Crombie in Montreal citing, in response to a demand for an explanation why a silk train had been late leaving Vancouver, reasons that he thought justified the train's being late. Moreover, the train had made up some of the time across the prairies and into Ontario. He argued that he had been advised that the schedule should have been lengthened because of heavy rains east of Edmonton. He then added what he thought was the clinching argument:

> I am quite sure that every officer and employee is alive to the necessity to make schedule time with these trains, consistent with safety, but when Roadmasters put out slow orders on certain portions of the track, that they consider unsafe for high speed, I think you will agree that should a derailment occur at one of these points, through ignoring the slow order, we would leave ourselves open to very severe criticism.

Nevertheless, tilting continued between officials in the office and those on the spot. About the same time as the previous exchange of niceties occurred, the Assistant General Manager in Vancouver was worrying about speed restrictions on track at that time of the year. He was angry about someone not telling him as directed about track conditions between Jasper and Vancouver. He said that speed restrictions were "rather numerous, particularly on the Yale and Ashcroft sub-divisions." He instructed J.H. McKinnon, Superintendent, Kamloops, the recipient of his letter of 27, July, 1927, personally to review all the slow orders still in force on the Kamloops division. He emphasized: ". . . it is imperative that the speed limitations be reduced to the minimum consistent with safe operation."

He continued:

> It is altogether probable your enquiry will develop that several of the orders can be removed and that in the case of others conditions will permit of the speed restriction being increased without incurring undue hazard . . . . The subject is one calling for very careful consideration and I shall look to receive a detailed report at an early date.

Letters and memoranda of which the above is an example take us behind the coolly efficient facade of an operating railway to reveal the anxiety that sometimes lay below surface appearances.

Concern continued to be expressed by Winnipeg authorities. Mr. W.A. Kingsland, General Manager of the CNR stationed in Winnipeg, and seemingly ranking official in the west, spoke and wrote temperately, trying always to ease situations that might otherwise get out of hand. On 21, December, 1927, he wrote an Inter-Departmental letter to J.R. Cameron, Assistant General Manager, Vancouver, with copies to the General Superintendents in Edmonton, Saskatoon, and Winnipeg, entitled *Silk Train Performance*. He started by saying that the Traffic Department was concerned at the "gradual increase in the time required to handle silk trains between termini and it is pointed out that this increase is seriously endangering our continuing to hold a share of this traffic." His second paragraph was of a specific nature:

> Notwithstanding the contention of the Traffic Department, I feel that one of the main essentials in traffic of this nature is that we should not attempt to do anything of a reckless character. With this in view, I firmly believe we should retain the winter schedule we have set up. . . . Admittedly there is a certain measure of risk in moving a train at any speed, but I am very anxious that all concerned should give the handling of this traffic most careful consideration and close attention so that the schedule we have set up for the winter period will be absolutely maintained, and all delays eliminated.

Again, one senses the importance of the twin objectives of speed with safety. Mr. Kingland concludes:

> It is of the utmost importance that we permanently retain this most lucrative traffic. . . .

CHAPTER NINE — THE LUCRATIVE TRADE

How lucrative, then, was the silk trade? The chart printed on page 71 is as comprehensive a set of statistics as one will find. It was issued in 1933 by the Traffic Bureau of The Silk Association of America, the main importing agency for silk in the United States, representing all the silk importers. It gives statistics for nine of the most active years of railway involvement in the transcontinental transportation of silk. The statistics cover the years 1924 to 1932 inclusive. The figures for 1922 cover the first quarter of the year only. The statistics affected all west coast ports of entry, both Canadian and American. According to this chart, the railways carried a peak aggregate of 522,347 bales of silk in 1928.

Silk was imported primarily through three west coast ports, with Seattle usually the busiest in the trade followed by Vancouver, and then San Francisco. Much lesser amounts of silk were imported through Los Angeles and Portland. Under the columns for each port, the annual percentage of the total silk imports is given for each year. The freight rate per 100 pounds is noted in the second last column.

Until 1931, all railroads charged a silk trade freight rate of $9.00 per hundred pounds. When the rate was finally changed in 1932, they agreed on a common tariff of $6.00 a hundred. The last column gives the total rail earnings for each year.

The lower sets of columns are highly significant. The figures for the trade through the Panama Canal are an unpleasant augury of things to come. The consequences of the growth of the Panama trade will be discussed in detail later.

Notice how valuable the silk trade was to both Canadian railways in 1927, the year in which they carried the most silk. Their total was 154,140 bales, or 30% of the aggregate. The gross amount earned through the silk trade for all railroads in the year was $6,465,324.60 for which the Canadian share was $1,939,597.35. This amount had to be divided between the Canadian Pacific Railway and the Canadian National Railways, with the former getting the larger portion. The silk trade was sufficiently important for Canadian National officials in their memoranda and letters to say often how necessary it was for them to keep their proportion of the "lucrative trade."

Both the Canadian and American dollars were worth very much more during the nineteen-twenties and the nineteen-thirties than they are today. Another economic circumstance important for an understanding of the times is that a disastrous stock market crash occurred in 1929 that precipitated a devastating downturn in business, industry, and employment. This became known as the Great Depression. It decimated the market for a luxury commodity like silk.

MP 4.1833

RAW SILK ARRIVALS

OVERLAND - RAIL MOVEMENT

	SEATTLE		SAN FRANCISCO		VANCOUVER		LOS ANGELES		PORTLAND		TOTAL RAIL (all ports)	% OF TOTAL ARRIVALS	OVERLAND RATE per 100 lbs.	ESTIMATED RAIL Earnings in Dollars
	Bales	% of all Rail	Bales	% of all Rail	Bales	% of all Rail	Bales	% of all Rail	Bales	% of all Rail				
1924	248,084	65.0	46,621	12.2	86,926	22.8	-	-	-	-	381,631	98.4	$9.00	$4,808,550.60
1925	231,543	50.5	99,082	21.6	128,247	27.9	-	-	-	-	458,872	93.7	9.00	5,781,787.20
1926	252,540	52.7	107,210	22.4	119,077	24.9	-	-	-	-	478,827	95.0	9.00	6,033,220.20
1927	241,081	47.0	117,900	23.0	154,140	30.0	-	-	-	-	513,121	92.9	9.00	6,465,324.60
1928	245,278	47.0	133,224	25.5	143,845	27.5	-	-	-	-	522,347	92.2	9.00	6,581,572.20
1929	231,998	44.6	144,216	27.7	133,796	25.7	-	-	10,438	2.0	520,448	78.7	9.00	6,557,644.80
1930	120,129	35.3	109,890	32.3	101,102	29.7	7,292	2.1	2,241	.7	340,654	62.0	9.00	4,292,240.40
1931	74,402	32.2	70,417	30.5	76,617	33.2	9,649	4.2	-	-	231,085	38.1	9.00	2,911,671.00
1932	70,621	31.9	63,009	28.4	68,638	31.0	19,290	8.7	-	-	221,558	40.5	6.00	1,861,087.20
1933*	5,629	38.1	3,910	26.5	3,798	25.7	1,440	9.7	-	-	14,777	15.0	6.00	124,126.80

	PANAMA CANAL ORIENT-N.Y.				SUEZ CANAL		EUROPEAN		TOTAL ARRIVALS (OVERLAND, PANAMA, SUEZ AND EUROPEAN) BALES
	Bales	% of Total Arrivals	Rate per 100 lbs.	Estimated Earnings in Dollars	Bales	% of Total Arrivals	Bales	% of Total Arrivals	
1924	130	.0	$9.00	$1,638.00	140	.0	5,774	1.5	387,675
1925	12,613	2.6	9.00	158,923.80	7,727	1.6	10,422	2.1	489,634
1926	7,607	1.5	9.00	95,848.20	11,420	2.3	6,346	1.3	504,200
1927	16,640	3.0	9.00	209,664.00	19,959	3.6	2,721	.5	552,441
1928	31,319	5.5	9.00	394,619.40	8,629	1.5	4,083	.7	566,378
1929	116,496	17.6	6.00	978,566.40	12,207	1.8	12,460	1.9	661,611
1930	190,061	34.6	6.00	1,596,512.40	1,606	.3	17,563	3.2	549,884
1931	351,474	58.0	6.00	2,952,381.60	407	.1	22,953	3.8	605,919
1932	311,757	57.0	6.00	2,618,758.80	330	.1	13,550	2.5	547,195
1933*	82,673	83.7	6.00	694,453.20	-	-	1,330	1.3	98,780

*January-February-March

TRAFFIC BUREAU
THE SILK ASSOCIATION OF AMERICA, INC.
468 FOURTH AVENUE, NEW YORK CITY

Over

Published by kind permission of **National Archives of Canada.**
RG30, CNR Records.

Over the years, almost every conceivable factor affecting the silk trade was examined in tedious detail. In a Canadian National inter-departmental letter written from Kamloops on 9, March, 1927, a curious problem of silk train management was raised. The heading of the letter referred to: *Divisional Meeting - discussion re fire protection combination coach on silk train.* The letter was sent from the Divisional Superintendent in Kamloops to J.R. Cameron. Assistant General Manager, Vancouver.

The letter referred to "colonist" cars that were made of wood, or wooden cars that were half baggage car and half passenger car being attached to silk trains for the accommodation of crew and security men who travelled with the trains. It should be explained that "colonist" cars were used in the early years of the twentieth century to carry immigrants, otherwise "colonists", across the country. These colonist cars had hard, uncushioned, often slatted wooden seats, but they also had a stove in a little room at the end of the car that burned coal and was used for cooking. It was these stoves that worried the superintendent at Kamloops. He wrote to Mr. Cameron:

> In discussing fire protection, at the divisional meeting held here February 22nd, the question of the combination baggage car and coach used for the accommodation of train crews and others on Silk Trains was brought up. It was pointed out that this car is equipped with oil lamps, and with an ordinary caboose stove, and in the event of an

accident to a silk train in which this car might be overturned or damaged while lamps were lit or when there was a fire in the stove, a serious fire would almost certainly result. . . .

In view of the hazard to valuable silk shipments, it was considered that some action should be taken to remedy the condition mentioned, by equipping this coach with electric lights and furnishing it with a safety type stove.

Nothing more was heard about this recommendation. It remains a curiosity in the saga of the silk trains.

A new twist to an old problem generated a memorandum from the Superintendent of Transportation to C.W. Tourtellotte, Assistant to Pacific Coast Manager, Canadian National Steamships, Vancouver. The date was 16, July, 1931. In it, the superintendent complained that the Vancouver booking agent did not know that silk was arriving on the night boat from Victoria to make connection with the crack Canadian National transcontinental passenger train, "The Continental." As a result, the general baggage for the train arrived before the silk so that The Continental was delayed in leaving Vancouver for the East. This reference is one of the few intimations we have that in the latter days of the silk trade, as at the beginning, silk travelled in cars attached to passenger trains. The Superintendent made the point:

"The Continental" is our only transcontinental train this year and is an exceedingly heavy train, and we are doing our utmost to eliminate every avoidable delay in order that she may be kept on time and would request the close cooperation of your department.

The "Lucrative Trade" was indeed in danger. We have seen that 1928 had been the high point of volume with 522,347 bales for all railways on the North American continent. In 1929, the year of the stock market crash, the volume was minimally less, but the decline of volume in 1930 was another matter. In that year the total number of bales carried was 340,654. The trade fell off even more sharply in subsequent years. Part of this decline was due to the persistent depression that followed the stock market crash of 1929, but a second important influence was the rapid growth of sea transport of silk through the Panama Canal.

Competition for a dwindling supply of silk had predictable results. The Canadian National and the Canadian Pacific had competed vigorously against one another for the silk that entered through Vancouver, but they stood together against the competition of ports and railways of the United States. By 1931, competition with U.S. railways was becoming keener. R.J. Foreman, Traffic Manager, C.N.R., Montreal, wrote a memorandum to D. Crombie, also in Montreal, calling his attention to one aspect of the growing competition. His memorandum, dated 7, May,

1931, was entitled: *Minimum Number of Bales of Silk Required / For Special Train Service.* Mr. Foreman wrote:

> The question of the number of bales of raw silk required for movement before special silk train would be operated was discussed at a meeting of the Traffic Executive Officers of all trans-continental lines held in Chicago on April 9th, and it was finally agreed to re-affirm an agreement that, apparently, had been in effect for a number of years as to a minimum of 800 bales of raw silk being necessary before special train service would be given.
>
> We did not know there was such an agreement in effect until the conference mentioned was held in Chicago last month. Both the Canadian Lines were represented at the meeting referred to, Mr. Kirkpatrick for the Canadian Pacific Railway and myself for the Canadian National Railways.

The final paragraph of this memorandum is the most important:

> While it is true up to recently at least, we have not operated any special silk trains from Vancouver for less that 1,000 raw bales neither have the Canadian Pacific Railway, the movement of this raw silk traffic is becoming so highly com-

petitive that both the Canadian Pacific Railway and ourselves consider we have to meet the practices of the U.S. Lines, in regard to this matter, if we expect to continue to have this traffic move via the Port of Vancouver in connection with either of our rail lines east of that port, more especially as the Great Northern Railway are now handling silk eastbound from Vancouver ex the N.Y.K. Line steamers (Japanese ships) that are docking at that port, and in doing so, will be governed by the agreement in respect to the minimum number of bales required before operating special trains, as outlined above.

The Great Northern Railroad, a line owned in the United States, now the Burlington Northern, operated then, as it does now, from Seattle to Vancouver. It was especially galling for both Canadian railways to have business they had looked upon as theirs stolen under their noses from their own port by an American competitor. Clearly, it the Canadian lines were operating on the basis of 1,000 bales being the minimum for a special train, and the Great Northern was using 800 bales as a minimum, an American train would be able to pull out of a station before the Canadian company had enough bales to form a train.

The fact is that the comfortable old ways of doing business were breaking down as there was less silk to transport and hence more competition. We have already seen that the C.N.R.'s crack transcontinental passenger train, The Continental, was held late in Vancouver on 16, July, 1931, waiting for silk. This happening was not unique and may have been one way the Canadian National moved the silk in a hurry when it did not have sufficient bales for a special train.

There is a memorandum dated 8, June, 1932, from E.C. Spalding, Foreign Freight Agent, CNR, Vancouver, to a senior official, E.T. Chappell, also in Vancouver. Mr. Spalding said that unloading crews could be arranged more cheaply and efficiently ". . . if we did not require the silk loaded rapidly to connect with our passenger train." The Harbour Board had said that then ". . . they would only employ a sufficient number of men so that the work would last the full two hours that they are required to pay." "As it is", said Mr. Spalding, "we seem to be paying more than is justifiable, as we already . . . pay the loading cost on the basis of 80 cents per ton which is double the ordinary charge for loading freight, and in the case under review, we seem to have paid on this weight basis considerable more that the actual outlay for labour cost."

CHAPTER TEN — CREW CHANGE AT WINNIPEG

The executive officers of the railways in their continental offices in Vancouver, Winnipeg, or Montreal might worry about the diminishing quantities of silk, or the rise in transportation costs per bale, but such concerns were far from the minds of the men with the operational responsibility of moving the silk fast from one coast to the other.

The writer's father was one of these men, working out of Winnipeg on the Canadian National. I remember the air of suppressed excitement in our home when my father was called to "fire" the engine of a silk train east of Winnipeg. I did not usually pay much attention to my father's "calls" to work, having learned to take them as routine. Silk trains were different. The conversation between my father and my mother seemed more highly charged when he talked about the silk train run. For one thing, the call was for three hours and not the usual two. He had to be on the shop track at the sprawling Fort Rouge yards of the Canadian National — one of the biggest in Canada — fully two hours before the silk train was expected. The engine crew checked the steam gauge, oiled and greased the engine, saw that the tender had been to the coal dock and that the water tank was full. No sooner had the silk train arrived than its old engine was disconnected and the new one put in place. Yard men quickly inspected every car to ensure that journals were ship-shape and that there were no hot boxes or any other obvious faults. Within a few minutes, the train was away, clacking over the numerous switching points leading to the Union Station near the heart of Winnipeg. The train did not stop but moved through the station with the connecting rods of the engine driving the train smoothly forwards, on its way to the Canadian Shield area of north-western Ontario. There the train squealed around the innumerable curves, bad enough, but not nearly so hair-raising as those through the Western Mountains.

As a boy, I imagined Canadian Pacific and Canadian National silk trains actually racing each other across the continent, sometimes almost side by side, with black smoke streaming back from the straining engines. Of course, it was not so romantic as that. If I had thought about it, I would have realized that could not have been the case. The silk usually came from different ships, landed at Vancouver at different times, often on different days. What was important was the elapsed time across the continent. Shippers and receivers were very much aware which railways, Canadian or American, made the best time in carrying the silk to New York, and sometimes to cities in between.

The Canadian National expected that its easier grades across the continent would help it counteract the Canadian Pacific's shorter distance. It has nothing like the Canadian Pacific's spiral tunnel through the Rocky Mountains to contend with. The Canadian National travelled the longer route as it crossed

CPR Locomotive #2334 on the turn-table before the roundhouse at Ottawa West, 1948.

*Published by kind permission of **National Archives of Canada**.*
Negative No. PA127204.

the northern prairies through Edmonton and Saskatoon while the Canadian Pacific's more southerly route passed through Calgary and Regina. The C.P.R. route often paralleled the international boundary with the United States at no great distance from it. Once the lines of both railways debouched onto the prairies from the Mountain defiles, there were few natural hazards to slow the trains until the Ontario border. It was on the prairies that the silk trains made their best speed.

CPR Marshalling Yards, Winnipeg.

Published by kind permission of **National Archives of Canada**.
Negative No. PA41494.

CHAPTER ELEVEN — THE SILK TRAINS WIND DOWN

With the advent of the nineteen thirties, the great days of the Canadian silk trade were drawing to a close. For years, competition had been intensifying. We have already noticed that worried C.N.R. officials constantly spurred their employees to greater efforts of efficiency, speed, and safety.

The deep economic depression, heralded by the stock market crash of 1929, continued unabated through most of the nineteen-thirties. Some significant figures for the silk trade are repeated below:

	Bales of Silk ALL RAILWAYS	Bales VIA PANAMA	TOTAL
1928	522,347	31,319	553,666
1929	520,448	116,496	636,944
1930	340,654	190,061	530,715
1931	231,085	351,474	582,559
1932	221,558	311,757	533,315

The crucial trend is the growth in the shipment of silk to New York via the all-water route.

Although all railways that carried silk had competed vigorously amongst themselves for a greater share of the trade, they closed ranks against the Panama threat. Railroaders knew that by 1928 steamship companies taking silk by the Panama route had reduced their freight rates from $9.00 a hundred pounds to $6.00 a hundred but the railways took no action then. However, so far as the silk importers were concerned, that reduction in freight cost alone justified importing silk via the all-water route. The railway freight rate remained at $9.00 a hundred pounds, but not for want of attempts to change it.

Apart from economic conditions and differing freight rates, one other important factor in diverting silk from Pacific Coast ports to the Panama Canal was that the Nippon Yusen Kaisha Steamship Line of Japan decided that it was about time to keep the distribution of Japanese silk in Japanese hands. The N.Y.K. Line designed and built a number of ". . . fast freighters to sail direct to New York by way of the Panama Canal."

The first of these new ships entered service in 1929. In that year the railways were getting 90% of the Trans Pacific silk trade. ". . . By 1939, the NYK ships had captured 90% of the silk trade." A complete reversal of percentages in 10 years!

*(Above quotations from W.K. Lamb, **Empress Odyssey**, in B.C. Historical Quarterly, January, 1948, page 38.)*

This reversal occurred despite the fact that it took about thirty days for the silk to go from Yokohama to New York by ship and only 15 or 16 days for it to go by ship to the Pacific Coast and about another 4 days for it to go from there to New York by train. It had always been assumed that raw silk deteriorated rapidly. If that had been true, clearly the Japanese had found a way to slow its deterioration. Perhaps the temperature at which it was carried was critical.

It had also been said that the sooner the new crop of silk reached the importers, the better the quality, The figures do not show a crop available in certain months but not in others. The Canadian National tabulation of silk received in the months of 1930, issued 15, January, 1931, and entitled *Silk Importations to the United States* shows a relative falling off in imports for May and June, but even in those months, the silk deliveries were considerable. The C.N.R. tabulations mentioned are printed on the succccding page.

Another argument justifying the pattern of shipping silk by sea and rail was that the importers in the eastern United States did not have sufficient storage space to accept ship-load quantities of raw silk. If this argument ever had any validity, it had ceased to be valid by the time N.Y.K. ships began to arrive in New York with large cargoes of silk. By then, the National Silk Exchange in New York had added storage facilities there.

Silk Importations to the United States.
-Bales-

	Total.	All-Rail.	% of Total.	Via Panama	% of Total
1928	553,826	522,507	94	31,319	6
1929	636,943	520,447	82	116,496	18
1930 - Jan.	45,154	27,268	60	17,886	40
Feb.	41,194	25,051	61	16,143	39
Mar.	37,884	23,820	63	14,064	37
Apr.	35,065	28,495	81	6,570	19
May	20,509	15,670	76	4,839	24
June	20,206	15,613	77	4,593	23
July	45,413	37,077	82	8,336	18
Aug.	49,533	39,638	80	9,895	20
Sept.	56,696	32,466	58	24,230	42
Oct.	64,419	30,657	48	33,762	52
Nov.	59,599	32,441	54	27,158	46
Dec.	63,685	35,451	57	28,234	43
Total for Year 1930:	539,357	343,647	64	195,710	36

Office of Gen. Frt. Traf. Mgr., Mtl., January 15, 1931.

Published by kind permission of National Archives of Canada. RG30, CNR Records.

Apart from experiencing the reality rather than just the threat of Japanese steamship competition, another economic blow was the calamitous decline in the value of silk in the course of ten years. The following table gives the picture as revealed by an authority:

> 1924 Average price for silk — $6.50 per pound.
> 1929 Average price for silk — $5.11 per pound.
> 1930 Average price for silk — $3.70 per pound.
> 1934 Average price for silk — $1.27 per pound.

The situation became an urgent matter when in September, 1929. The Blue Funnel Steamship Line was unable to get any raw silk from Canton, China, for the Canadian National because lower freight rates were being quoted by ships sailing to San Francisco. Also, the fast, new motorship service from China to New York by way of the Panama Canal was attracting the bulk of the raw silk. Something had to be done fast.

The one real advantage that the railways had over the all-water route was that the latter took almost twice as long to get to the Atlantic seaboard. That raised the cost of insurance which was usually quoted on a per diem basis. It was thought that if the railways could agree on a freight rate reduction similar to that granted by the steamship companies, perhaps the railways could again become competitive and win back a substantial portion of the silk trade.

CHAPTER TWELVE — A QUESTION OF RATES

On, 6, March, 1930, R.W. Long, General Freight Traffic Manager of the Canadian National, based in Montreal, wrote a four-page letter to Mr. R.L. Burnap, Vice-President of the Canadian National, also in Montreal, explaining in detail what the problem was, the options for the company in dealing with it, and setting forth strategies for achieving agreement amongst all those concerned.

Mr. Long's second paragraph stated the essential question:

> As you know, the question of rates on silk from Pacific Coast ports to New York has been engaging the attention of the Trans-Continental Executives since last spring. They have been watching the developments in connection with the movement of this traffic via the Panama Canal and it is apparent that they are now concerned because of the increased volume of business which is being handled via that route.

Mr. Long then explained that no one seemed to have been able to "determine definitely the measure of the disadvantage involved in Panama Canal routing." It was known that the transportation costs by rail were $9.00 per 100 pounds and via the Panama Canal at that time, so it was alleged, as low as $3.00 per hundred pounds, but that did not tell the whole story.

R.J. Foreman, a colleague of Mr. Long's, had calculated that with the extra interest payments estimated at $1.00 a pound, and extra insurance estimated at 50 cents per pound, the true transportation costs by way of the Panama were $4.50 per pound as contrasted with the sea and rail costs of $9.00 a pound. Mr. Long acknowledged that the lesser costs would naturally appeal to the silk dealers.

The Canadian National men had discussed the situation with their opposite numbers on the Canadian Pacific. Mr. Long reported to Mr. Burnap:

> Mr. Foreman has also discussed the matter with Mr. Kirkpatrick of the Canadian Pacific, and he is under the impression that because of their larger interests, the Canadian Pacific are very much concerned. Under present conditions, San Francisco is the preferred Pacific Coast port for the handling of this silk, by reason of the fact that if cargoes are discharged at San Francisco, the all-rail route as well as the most frequent service through the Canal is available. This means attracting the

business as against Vancouver, which, you can appreciate, is looked upon quite seriously by the Canadian Pacific, and based on Mr. Kirkpatrick's attitude, Mr. Foreman is under the impression that they have about made up their minds that a reduction in the all-rail rate is necessary if the business is to be retained for the all-rail carriers as heretofore.

That was the nub of the question, but Mr. Long was not convinced that a reduction in the all-rail rate would not be followed by a reduction in the all-water rate. He therefore suggested specific contracts with those who arranged shipment for the silk to stabilize the volume so far as the railways were concerned. Neither Mr. Long nor Mr. Foreman, however, believed that such proposed contracts, which would necessarily involve agreement with the Trans-Pacific Steamship Lines, could, in the end, prove practicable. Mr. Long pointed out that such contracts might not even be desirable from the Canadian National's point-of-view because, as the Canadian Pacific had its own steamships, these contracts " . . . would put a considerable control of the routing of this silk in the hands of the Trans-Pacific Steamship Lines, in which event we figure that the Canadian Pacific would increase their advantage to the detriment of our line." There were questions, then, of self interest that had to be accommodated within the larger solution, if it existed, that affected all railways.

Mr. Long, finally, summarized his and Mr. Foreman's recommendation:

> Our view is, therefore, that if the other trans-continental rail lines have about reached the conclusion that something should be done in the way of a reduced rail rate to offset the Panama Canal competition, Chairman Toll should be authorized by the Traffic Executives of such lines to negotiate best possible rate, having in mind the spread between the Panama Canal rate and the all-rail rate prevailing prior to the increased competition from one cause or another...."

Mr. Long then said that there was going to be a meeting of the Traffic Executive Officers of the transcontinental lines in Chicago in the following week. As Mr. Kirkpatrick of Canadian Pacific was going to be present, Mr. Long suggested that Mr. Foreman and possibly he himself should attend the meeting.

Next, Mr. Long asked one of his officials how much the Canadian National would lose, based on 1929 silk tonnage, if the freight rate was reduced from $9.00 to $6.00 a hundred pounds. On 28, March, 1930, the answer came back that the revenue reduction would be about $211,902.00, a considerable sum in 1930 dollars.

The meeting in mid-March, 1930, to which Mr. Long referred, may have resulted in a letter dated 10, April, 1930, from L.E. Oliphant, Chairman, Trans-Continental Advisory Committee, to all members of that committee, asking them to consider, at their May, 1930 meeting, a proposal to decrease the freight rates on silk coming from the Pacific Coast, from $9.00 a hundred pounds to $6.00 a hundred. The proposal had been on the agenda of the April meeting of that committee, but because Central Freight Association carriers had not had an opportunity to consider that proposal beforehand, a decision was put off until the May meeting. In his letter, Mr. Oliphant quoted an earlier letter from Chairman Toll of the Central Freight Association, which, after saying that the silk rates had been a concern for that past year, continued:

> They (the Executive Traffic Officers) had hoped that the tendency on the part of some of the importers to switch this traffic to the Canal route would not result in seriously affecting the bulk of the movement, but results are steadily proving the contrary, and it appears evident that it would only be a short time until practically all the raw silk would be handled via the Canal. They, therefore, have concluded that rate of $6.00 is necessary to retain what we are now getting and to recover tonnage now moving via the canal.

The letter went on to say that it had been calculated that in total the rate by canal was in reality $6.00 by sea with interest $1.12 a hundred pounds. When insurance and drayage were added to that, the total transportation costs by the Canal would be $8.75 per hundred pounds. To the proposal by rail of $6.00 a hundred would have to be added the sea transport from the Orient to the Pacific Coast ports of $3.00 per hundred, making a total of $9.00 per hundred, or very close to what the Canal rate was. Mr. Oliphant added that the total importation of silk was about 600,000 bales now weighing 140 pounds each.

Mr. Oliphant gave the percentage of raw silk reaching New York by rail and by canal. It showed a staggering change in proportions during the course of the year:

Because of the critical situation, Traffic Executives were asked for a decision as soon as possible. The letter added:

1929	% Overland	% via Canal
Jan. to June inclusive	92	8
July	93	7
August	89	11
September	73	27
October	61	39
November	69	31
December (Via San Francisco)	40	60
January, 1930 (Via San Francisco)	22	78

(See also the bar Graph from the Silk Association of America printed on the next page.)

The proposal has been submitted to the secretary of the Silk Association, and we have advice from him that the proposed rate as well as ten hour lengthening of the schedule for passenger train service is satisfactory to the Silk Association.

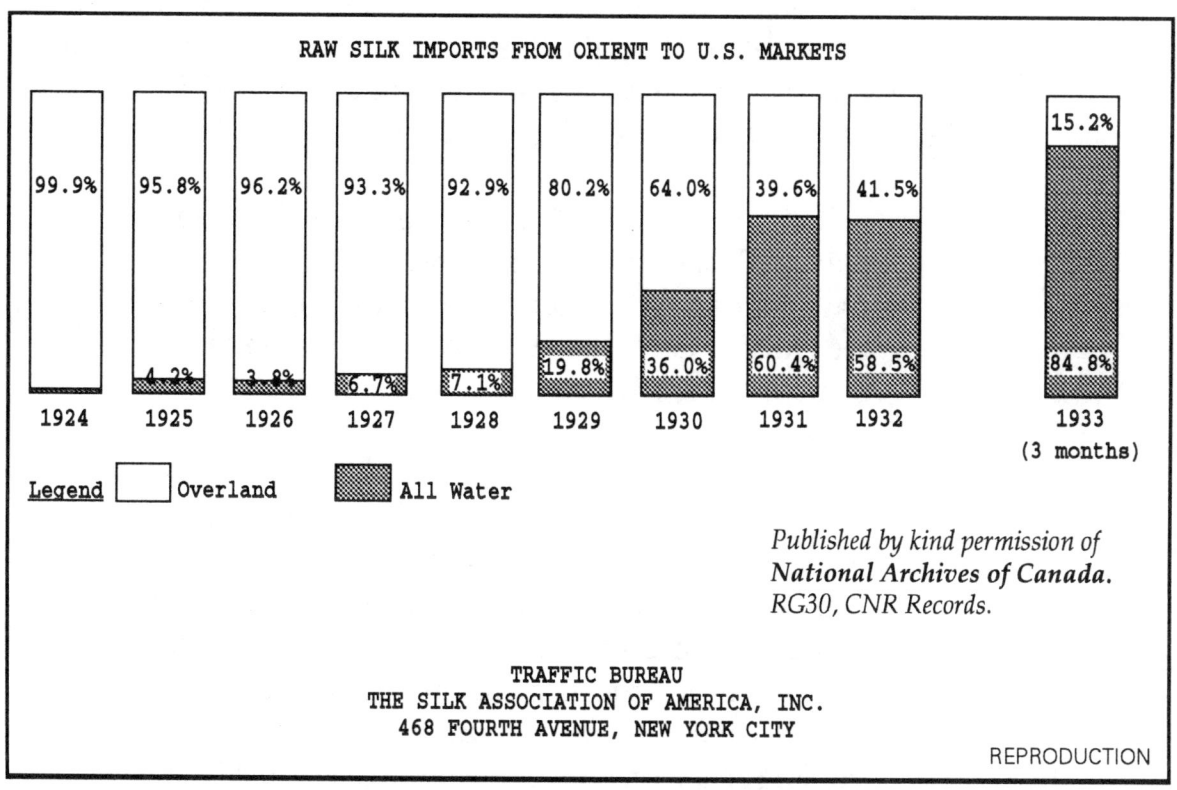

With the falling off in the silk trade, it was no longer possible always to run special silk trains. The concession of the longer time required to get the silk across the continent was an acknowledgement of this fact and a recognition by all concerned that when the silk cars had to be part of a passenger train, the silk would not get to New York so quickly as when it travelled in its own trains.

Despite the urgent need to cut the freight rates, that did not happen at the May meeting of the railway rate representatives. The situation became worse rather than better. In exasperation, on 16, September, 1930, the Silk Association of America issued a press release which, under the heading, *SILK RATE ATTITUDE OF RAILROADS IS HIT*, reported as follows:

> Failure of the Trans-Continental railroads to meet the rapidly increasing competition of the all-water route for Raw Silk shipments from the Orient through the Panama Canal has aroused strong resentment and outspoken surprise from Raw Silk officials in this market.
>
> Paolino Gerli, Chairman of the Raw Silk division of the Silk Association of America, Inc., and Vice-President and General Manager of E. Gerli & Co., Inc., expresses wonder that the railroads should deliberately jeopardize the most lucrative class of business that they have so long enjoyed, by stubbornly withholding action on rate reductions that are inevitable, he says, if the roads do not wish to permanently lose the business.

The Silk Association explained why, in its opinion, no rate reduction had taken place. "The Western railroads had seen the justice of the arguments, but it is the Eastern Lines, such as the Pennsylvania, the Erie, and the Lackawanna who have steadfastly taken the intransigent attitude of charging all the traffic will bear. Thirty to thirty-five day service from the Orient to New York by all water route is in the offing", concluded Mr. Gerli, "and with it the Railroads stand to lose revenue freight equal to $6,000,000 annually."

The United States had no railroads operating under a single name that carried passengers and freight from the Pacific to the Eastern Coast, as did both the Canadian Pacific and the Canadian National. Traditionally, a railroad like the Sante Fe or the Union Pacific would work the western United States but end at Chicago. Similarly, eastern railroads tended not to go west of Chicago. Undoubtedly, western railroads had trade agreements with eastern railroads to allow their cars and the silk trains to run over their lines. The United States railroads that wanted a reduction in the silk rates were the western railroads where the silk runs originated. The Eastern railroads were not the originating carriers for raw silk, or were rarely so. Thay did not want to breach the freight rate structure in case concessions for raw silk would lead to concessions being demanded for all kinds of merchandise.

Mr. R.J. Foreman, Traffic Manager of the Canadian National, sent a copy of the news release of 16, September, 1930, to his superior, Mr. R.W. Long. He told Mr. Long that on the very day the news release appeared in the *New York Daily News Record*, another meeting of the Trans-Continental Executive Committee had been held in Chicago, but that committee meeting, too, had taken no action on the demand for a silk rate reduction. He said, "the Trunk Lines had definitely turned down the application for reduction in this rate."

On 13, October, 1930, about a month later, Mr. Long wrote Mr. Foreman requesting information about the degree to which the Panama Canal was diverting raw silk from the railways. The next day, Mr. Foreman replied setting forth the following table:

PANAMA CANAL		
	JAPAN	CHINA
Year,1928	28,209 bales	3,110 bales
Year,1929	91,508 bales	24,988 bales
Jan.,1930	13,843 bales	4,043 bales
Feb.,1930	13,653 bales	2,490 bales
Mar.,1930	10,253 bales	3,811 bales
Apr.,1930	4,317 bales	2,253 bales
May.,1930	3,117 bales	1,722 bales
Jun.,1930	1,430 bales	3,163 bales
Jul.,1930	2,212 bales	6,124 bales
Aug.,1930	4,161 bales	5,734 bales
Sep.,1930	18,780 bales	5,450 bales

Mr. Foreman added:

> You will note from the above figures that in spite of the generally decreased movement of Oriental silk into the U.S., there had been a large increase in the movement via the Panama Canal, and with the new fast service of the N.Y.K. Line to the Eastern seaboard, the situation respecting the movement via the Panama Canal will probably tend to become more acute than in the past.

In another inter-departmental letter dated 15, December, 1930, on the subject of movement of silk through the Panama Canal, Mr. Foreman sent Mr. Long a table showing the imports of silk into the United States for the month of November, 1930 — this time showing the volume of raw silk entering the ports of western North America, and, therefore, that quantity of silk that would travel to New York by rail.

Mr. Long derived the proportions by rail and the Panama Canal as follows: rail: 54.4%; Panama: 45.6% and entered these percentages on Mr. Foreman's letter in pencil over his signature.

IMPORT OF RAW SILK INTO THE UNITED STATES November, 1930		
VIA PORT OF:	JAPAN	CHINA
Seattle	6,448 bales	819 bales
San Francisco	10,228 bales	941 bales
Vancouver	8,860 bales	536 bales
Portland	N/A bales	N/A bales
Los Angeles	4,459 bales	150 bales
TOTALS	29,995 bales	2,446 bales
VIA PANAMA CANAL	25,307 bales	1,851 bales

Still another meeting was held in Chicago, this time on 9, April, 1931. As Mr. Foreman, who attended, reported to Mr. Long on 13, April 1931, the Traffic Executive Officers of the American railroads that carried most of the silk and therefore wanted the reduction, met during the morning of the Chicago meeting to try to arrive at an acceptable compromise. They said that they would be willing to accept another 48 hours of insurance charges after the silk arrived in New York, and that they would agree that the reduction in rates, if granted, would be of a temporary nature only, to be cancelled if the reduction did not result in more silk going by rail. When the full meeting met in the afternoon, the western men believed that they had a very persuasive package to offer the eastern people.

It was still not successful. When the proposal was submitted to a secret vote for all the representatives, it was turned down. The majority against making the reduction, was according to the chairman, considerable. As Mr. Foreman said, "(The result) was rather surprising to me." Mr. Foreman told Mr. Long that "It is impossible to say, of course, what Lines voted in favour of the reduction, and those that voted against it, but undoubtedly, some Lines voted on the proposition that were really not vitally interested in the traffic."

According to Mr. Foreman, all transcontinental lines' representatives now supported the proposal for a reduction of rates, although originally there had been some difference of opinion. He added: ". . . The Trans-Continental Lines had now unanimously reached the conclusion that the reduction was necessary if the proportion of this traffic that was still moving via the overland routes was to be retained" or increased. One of the additional arguments of those wishing the reduction had been that up to June, 1918, the rate per hundred pounds had been $4.00, rising thereafter to $7.50 per hundred. Clearly, there was nothing sacred about the $9.00 a hundred rate.

In another letter to Mr. Long, also on 13, April, 1930, Mr. Foreman revealed that at the meeting in question, some talk had taken place about increasing the minimum of 800 bales of raw silk necessary before "special passenger train service will be given" to 900 bales "or preferably 125,000 pounds — it being figured the bales weighed on an average of 140 lbs. . . . " Some representatives at the meeting did not want to decide this question at the time and the minimum for a special train remained at 800 bales.

Soon after receiving Mr. Foreman's letter about the meeting, Mr. Long summarized it and sent the summary to Mr. R.L Burnap, Vice-President of the Canadian National Railways. He concluded his summary by referring to the opinion of the Canadian Pacific: "As you know, the Canadian Pacific have been very much exercised because of the loss of this silk traffic and I do not believe that Mr. Stephen will view with any sympathy the action of the Traffic Executive Association."

The problem of the diversion of raw silk through the Panama Canal would not go away. Again the western Traffic Executives pressed their case for a rate reduction. There must have been much persuasion and lobbying behind the scenes. Finally, on November 27, 1931, the eastern representatives agreed to a reduction of the freight rate on silk from $9.00 to $6.00 a hundred pounds effective December 28, 1931. This reduction must have been conditional on a reversal of the trend of silk going to New York via the Panama, because, on the situation worsening, the rate by rail reverted to $9.00 per hundred on December 31, 1934.

CHAPTER THIRTEEN — TOO LITTLE, TOO LATE

While all this was going on, the railways continued to keep careful records about the handling of raw silk. On 28, September, 1932, the Japanese steamship *Norfolk Maru* unloaded a silk cargo in Vancouver. A silk train was ordered consisting of four silk cars and a colonist car for crew and escorts. A summary showed that the silk was discharged from the ship in one hour and twenty minutes; that the cars were loaded in two hours and five minutes; and that the elapsed time between discharging the silk began and the Canadian National train left the dock was three hours and ten minutes. The average loading time was forty-two minutes per car.

The various crews were maintaining their efficiency, but far less silk was coming to the port of Vancouver. The Canadian Pacific, therefore, stopped running silk trains after 1933. Instead, the C.P.R. began attaching a few cars laden with silk to regular passenger trains. Thus, an honourable Canadian Pacific service in the handling of silk that began in 1886, came to a little-noticed end in 1933.

Montreal officials of the Canadian National continued to keep track of the pattern of their silk movements. On 9, February, 1932, less than two months after the reduced rail tariff had gone info effect, before any results of that reduction were evident, Mr. Foreman prepared a summary "showing the import movement of Raw Silk, in bales, via the various Pacific Coast ports, thence overland rail, versus movement via the all-water route through the Panama Canal, for the years 1928 to 1931 inclusive, together with figures indicating the percentage of the total movement for the different years."
That summary follows:

	OVERLAND - ALL RAIL						
	VANCOUVER	SEATTLE	SAN FRANCISCO	PORTLAND	LOS ANGELES	TOTAL BALES	VIA PANAMA
1928	143,845	245,278	133,224	—	—	522,347	31,320
1929	133,796	231,998	144,216	10,438	—	520,448	116,496
1930	101,102	120,129	109,890	2,241	7,292	340,654	190,061
1931	76,617	74,402	70,417	—	—	221,436	351,474

PERCENTAGE OF TOTAL VIA THE PANAMA CANAL	
1928	5.6%
1929	18.2%
1930	35.8%
1931	61.3%

The handwriting was now on the wall for the overland rail route.

We have seen that the economic depression of the thirties reduced the world-wide demand for silk. The railroaders might have hoped that they could become competitive again when economic conditions returned to normal, but there was no clear direction in which they could move to make that happen. Moreover, the Second World War was just around the corner. Silk reached Canada until 1940, but when Japan attacked Pearl Harbour on 6, December, 1941, and the United States was immediately embroiled in war, the source of silk whether from Japan or China was abruptly cut off.

The end of the trade was prophetically signalled in an interdepartmental letter, dated 2, January, 1941, from F.E. Cary, Superintendent of Transportation, CNR, Vancouver, to W.T. Moodie, General Superintendent, Vancouver. This letter is re-printed in the Appendix. In part, it reads as follows:

For your information, total silk traffic handled by passenger trains from Vancouver during 1940 amounted to 504 pieces (88,229 pounds)

Totals for previous years are as follows:

1939 —   6,618 pieces
1938 — 13,609 pieces
1937 — 16,725 pieces
1936 — 13,847 pieces

It is not explained why, in this late memorandum, pieces and not bales are used as the standard of measurement. Each "piece" seemed to weigh about 175 pounds, for a total weight over the four years of about 4445 tons. At the old estimate of thirty tons to a car, that would mean only about 148 cars for the whole four year period. A far cry from the tonnage moved and the cars used in 1927, or during the great days of the silk trade for the decade 1922–1932.

Why did the silk trade not recover after the war ended in 1945? Much silk continues to be made into quality clothing. The likely answer is that most silk used today in the United States textile industry is probably imported more cheaply directly from the Orient by way of the Panama Canal.

On the other hand, silk substitutes have cut seriously into the traditional silk market. The first of these was rayon, invented as long ago as 1855, but slow to gain popularity. Nevertheless, 52,000,000 pounds of this cellulose-based material were manufactured as early as 1925.

No one would seriously mistake rayon for silk. The same could not be said for nylon which began to be produced in large quantities during the Second World War when real silk was not available. It was invented by the American firm of E.I. Du Pont de Nemours in 1935. The first factory was opened in the United States in 1940, just in time to earn its spurs during the war. Nylon was and is tough, with a beautiful sheen. It was so immediately popular that its name became a synonym for ladies' stockings. Nylons were about the most appreciated gift one could give a woman during those years of war. Nylon's popularity has endured. Today, it is made into the kind of garments for which silk was renowned. Now, of course, there are several other man-made textiles that rival silk. Foremost among these is the Polyester group.

⌘ ⌘ ⌘

During this account, we have discussed the origins of silk, the way it spread around the world in the days when transportation was much more difficult and primitive than it is today. We have considered how Canada became part of the network of silk distribution and, with the United States, contributed the silk trains to the continuing saga of silk.

Although we have reached the end of the silk train story, there are some of us, old enough to remember, who are still stirred by the romance of Canada's contribution to the silk trains that flourished during the age of Steam Railroading.

APPENDIX

1. Letter from George Olds, General Traffic Manager, CPR, to T. G. Shaughnessy, (after whom, the Shaughnessy Heights section of Vancouver was named), then Vice-President of the Canadian Pacific Railway, dated 17, September, 1892, regarding a mishap to a box car containing silk.

2. Statement of Canadian National silk trains bound for New York, July 1, 1925, to July 1, 1926.

3. Data about silk train ex S.S. Protesilaus March 17, 1931.

4. Letter to Mr. R.W. Long, Montreal, dated 28, March, 1930, giving Canadian National Revenue losses if silk rate reduced from $9.00 to $6.00 a hundred pounds.

5. Silk brought to Canadian National by Blue Funnel Ships, Calendar year, 1931.

6. Silk brought to Canadian National by Blue Funnel Ships, Calendar year, 1932.

7. Last CNR letter found in file, 2, January, 1941

8. CNR Silk Train on the move in British Columbia, about 1928.

9. Time-tables of Canadian Pacific Trans-Canada Trains, May, 1928.

Canadian Pacific Railway Company,
Office of General Traffic Manager

Geo. Olds,
Gen. Traffic Manager

Montreal, 17th September 1892.

T. G. Shaughnessy Esq,
Vice President.

Dear Sir:-

I beg to call your attention to the enclosed report from Mr. Kerr relative to the manner in which the "Empress of India's" silk cargo was handled.

The circumstance of car No. 4282 catching fire was, I assume, something beyond control, and no doubt you will approve Mr. Whyte's action in holding over at Winnipeg one day, cars 87182, 25916, and 13294, but the Traffic Department finds itself very much handicapped in the obtaining and holding of this traffic against the extraordinary prompt despatch given such property at, and all the way east of San Francisco to New-York.

I am informed that in the case of a large consignment ex the "Empress of Japan" the interest alone costs the consignee $50.00 per day 24 hours. You will see from this how anxious consignees are always to obtain quick delivery. We obtained very little of this freight during the year ending June 1st 1892, but have received several large consignments since.

(T. G. S. No. 2.)

The last arrivals ex the "Empress of China" were the largest we have ever received in one ship; that we obtained so much for this ship was greatly owing to the fact that the "China" on her last voyage from Yokohama to San Francisco went to her destination via Panama and those who intended shipping their silk by her gave us the preference with the expectation of getting their property delivered quicker. I very much fear they were disappointed.

Yours truly,

Geo. Olds -
General Traffic Manager.

Enclos.

Published by kind permission of Corporate Archives, **Canadian Pacific Railway.**

CANADIAN NATIONAL RAILWAYS
WESTERN REGION

Vancouver, B.C., 25th August 1926.

File Y 7330-6.

STATEMENT OF SILK TRAINS HANDLED AT VANCOUVER, B.C. FOR NEW YORK VIA CANADIAN NATIONAL RAILWAYS & CONNECTIONS.

July 1st 1925 to July 1st, 1926
commencement of lease to renewal.

Date	Steamer	No. Bales of silk.	No. of cars.	Connecting Line.	Time Vancr- New York	Gross Earnings.
1925.						
July 1	Tyndareus	2379	8	D. & L.W.	86 hrs 23m	$29,840.09
" 28	Achilles	2158	9	N.Y.C.	91 hrs. -	27,382.26
Aug 17	Philoctetes	3338	11	Penn. R.R.	88 hrs 25m	41,658.82
Sep 9	Tyndareus	5256	14	D. & L.W.	89 hrs 11m	65,877.92
Oct 21	Achilles	2154	6	Erie R.R.	83 hrs 56m	26,832.03
Nov 3	Protesilaus	2907	8	N.Y.C.	87 hrs -	36,293.05
" 26	Philoctetes	3054	9	Penn. R.R.	91 hrs 09m	38,010.80
Dec 17	Tyndareus	2797	9	D. & L.W.	91 hrs 16m	34,897.46
1926.						
Feb 6	Ixion	1941	6	Erie R.R.	89 hrs 28m	24,651.31
" 17	Philoctetes	1721	6	N.Y.C.	90 hrs 48m	20,028.26
Mar 12	Tyndareus	1729	6	Penn. R.R.	91 hrs 49m	21,755.08
Apr 14	Protesilaus	2733	9	D. & L.W.	90 hrs 57m	35,151.70
" 29	Talthybius	1359	5	Erie R.R.	105 hrs 34m #	17,323.37
May 10	Philoctetes	3370	10	N.Y.C.	90 hrs 32m	42,175.72
Jun 10	Tyndareus	4348	13	Penn R.R.	94 hrs 55m	55,110.29
Total	15 steamers	41,217	129	-	-	516,988.16
Average	-	2748	9	-	90 hrs 49m	34,465.88

cars attached to train #4 ex Winnipeg.

*Published by kind permission of **National Archives of Canada**.*
RG30, CNR Records.

CANADIAN NATIONAL RAILWAYS

Vancouver, B. C. March 17th, 1931.

File - 6610-190.

Silk train ex s. s. "Protesilaus" March 17th, 1931 - 6 Cars.

Mr. B. T. Chappell - Bldg.

The following is the record of handling silk ex the s. s. "Protesilaus" March 17th:-

	Hour	Elapsed Time.
Ship docked	9.55 K	
Discharge silk commenced	10.32	37"
completed	12.06	1' 34"
Loading cars commenced	11.00	
completed	12.34	1' 34"
Train left Dock	12.38	04"
arrived our Yard	12.51	13"
Train left Vancouver	12.53	02"
Crew called for:		
Train crew	12.30	
Ships Gangs	10.30	
Car Gangs	11.00	
No. Hatches worked	1	
No. Car Gangs	6	
No. Ships Gangs	2	
Weather	Mild, Dull	

S u m m a r y

Time occupied discharging silk	1' 34"
Time occupied loading cars	1' 34"
Elapsed time commencement of discharge to departure from dock	2' 06"
Average time loading per car	15.6"

Supt. of Transportation.

*Published by kind permission of **National Archives of Canada**.*
RG30, CNR Records.

INTER-DEPARTMENTAL CORRESPONDENCE

Montreal, Que. Mar. 28, 1930.

SUBJECT: IMPORT RATES ON SILK.   OUR FILE: Y-75-7.

MAR 29 1930

Mr. R. W. Long, Montreal, Que.

In reply to your letter of March 17th, and confirming telephone conversation with Mr. Kember on the 25th instant.

In the event of the rate on Raw Silk from the Pacific Coast being reduced from $9.00 to $6.00 per 100 lbs, our loss of revenue based on the tonnage handled during 1929, would work out as follows:-

VIA VANCOUVER.
  6,562,939 lbs at $7.86 equals $515,847.00.

VIA CHICAGO.
  8,944,696 lbs at $1.34 equals $119,859.00.

             TOTAL $635,706.00.

From the above figures you will note that the total revenue amounts to $635,706.00, and inasmuch as the rate will be reduced one third, the loss of revenue would amount to $211,902.00.

These figures are subject to slight correction on account of the following assumptions having been made:-

(1) No deduction has been made for traffic lightered in New York Harbour.

(2) No allowance has been made for the portion of earnings accruing to the Hoboken Manufacturers Railroad, on traffic handled by them.

(3) Lines east of Chicago receive 27½% of the through rate, and out of this proportion we make varying settlements with the different trunk lines which range from 45.65% of the proportion east of Chicago, to 46.0%, and we have taken average of 45.8%.

*Published by kind permission of **National Archives of Canada**.
RG30, CNR Records.*

Silk ex Blue Funnel
Line Steamers Via Vancouver
1931

Steamer	Docked Vancouver	Weight (lbs)	Earnings
Tencer	Jan. 14	285,837	$25,725
Ixion	Feb. 4	191,675	26,254
Tyndareus	Feb. 24	89,421	8,048
Protesilaus	Mar. 17	260,672	28,467
Tencer	Apr. 7	93,615	8,425
Ixion	May 5	187,661	16,886
Tyndareus	May 25	230,190	20,720
Protesilaus	June 23	153,748	13,801
Ixion	July 21	173,966	15,657
Tyndareus	Aug. 17	264,426	23,798
Protesilaus	Sept. 15	178,995	12,492
Ixion	Oct. 13	178,622	12,425
Tyndareus	Nov. 10	122,913	11,062
Protesilaus	Dec. 14	98,546	5,187
		2,518,797	$228,947
		1264 tons	

Total	3,129,908
07	2,528,797
	601,111

Published by kind permission of National Archives of Canada.
RG30, CNR Records.

Silk ex Blue Funnel Line Steamers via Vancouver
1932

Steamer	Docket Vancouver	Weight (lbs)	Earnings
Ixion	Jan. 16	34,665	$ 2,080
Tyndareus	Feb. 10	234,085	14,025
Protesilaus	Mar. 8	142,513	8,560
Ixion	Apr. 6	79,224	4,859
Tyndareus	May 2	76,229	4,580
Protesilaus	May 29	83,420	5,006
Ixion	June 27	44,283	2,675

694,819 = $41,805
347 tons

Total - 1,276,484 lbs
B.F. 694,829 "
Other Lines 581,655 "

Published by kind permission of **National Archives of Canada.**
RG30, CNR Records.

INTER-DEPARTMENTAL CORRESPONDENCE

Vancouver, B. C., January 2, 1941.

YOUR FILE	SUBJECT	OUR FILE
	SILK SHIPMENTS	7330-9

Mr. W. T. Moodie
   General Superintendent
      Vancouver, B. C.

- - - - - - - - - - -

     For your information, total silk traffic handled by passenger trains from Vancouver during 1940 amounted to 504 pieces (88,229 pounds).

     Totals for previous years are as follows:

          1939 - 6,618 pieces
          1938 - 13,609 "
          1937 - 16,725 "
          1936 - 13,847 "

     It will be noted that there is a severe reduction in the volume of this traffic in 1940, this being due to war conditions, a reduction in freight rates encouraging movement by freight train rather than passenger train, and smaller volume of imported silk.

                                               Sup't of Transportation

c.c. Messrs: W. C. Owens - Winnipeg, Man.
             J. J. Behan   -   "   "

*Published by kind permission of **National Archives of Canada**.*
RG30, CNR Records..

CNR Silk Train on the move in British Columbia, about 1928.

Published by kind permission of **Canadian National Railways.** *Photo. No. 12986*

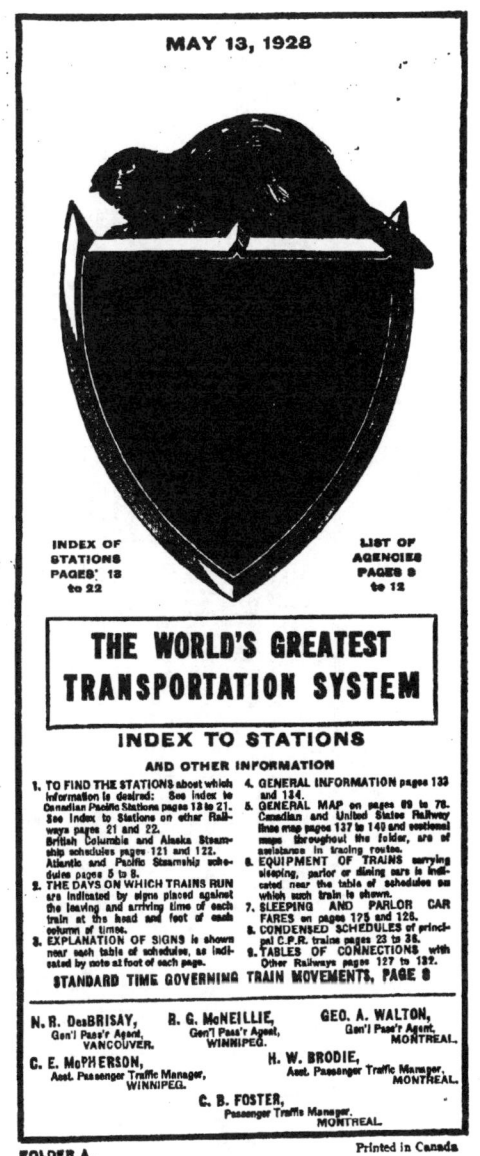

Published by kind permission of Corporate Archives, **Canadian Pacific Railway.**

TRANS-CANADA LIMITED
ALL-SLEEPING-CAR TRAIN

DAILY—WEST
No. 7—Montreal to Vancouver — Hrs. Mins. 89 15
Nos. 9-7—Toronto to Vancouver — 85 30

TABLE J

DAILY—EAST
No. 8—Vancouver to Montreal — Hrs. Mins. 88 30
Nos. 8-10—Vancouver to Toronto — 83 10

Effective May 13 to Sept. 29 from Montreal Toronto and Vancouver

Miles	Station	Time								
	Lv New York, N.Y.	9.45pm	E.T.	Sa	Su	M	Tu	W	Th	Fr
	Lv Boston, Mass.	9.00pm		Su	M	Tu	W	Th	Fr	Sa
	Lv Portland, Me.	8.10pm								
	Lv Saint John, N.B.	7.00pm		Sa	Su	M	Tu	W	Th	Fr
	Lv Quebec, Que.	12.30am		Su	M	Tu	W	Th	Fr	Sa
0.0	Lv Montreal	7.15pm		Su	M	Tu	W	Th	Fr	Sa
111.3	Ar Ottawa, Ont.	10.15pm								
	Lv Ottawa	10.30pm								
242.3	Ar Chalk River	2.00am		M	Tu	W	Th	Fr	Sa	Su
	Lv Chalk River	2.05am								
360.0	Ar North Bay	5.25am								
	Lv North Bay	5.30am								
439.0	Ar Sudbury	7.30am								
	Lv Toronto (Union)	8.00pm		Su	M	Tu	W	Th	Fr	Sa
	Ar MacTier No. 9	3.00am		M	Tu	W	Th	Fr	Sa	Su
	Lv MacTier	3.10am								
	Ar Sudbury	6.55am								
439.0	Lv Sudbury	7.45am								
472.9	Ar Cartier	9.00am								
	Lv Cartier	9.05am								
609.3	Ar Chapleau	1.10pm								
	Lv Chapleau	1.20pm								
741.1	Ar White River	5.15pm								
	Lv White River	5.20pm								
859.4	Ar Schreiber	8.50pm								
	Lv Schreiber	8.55pm								
987.9	Ar Port Arthur	12.35am	E.T.	Tu	W	Th	Fr	Sa	Su	M
992.3	Ar Fort William	12.55am								
	Lv Fort William	1.10am	C.T.							
1139.5	Ar Ignace	3.55am								
	Lv Ignace	4.05am								
1285.7	Ar Kenora	7.40am								
	Lv Kenora	7.50am								
1411.6	Ar Winnipeg, Man.	11.15am								
	Lv Winnipeg	11.45am								
1544.7	Ar Brandon	3.00pm								
	Lv Brandon	3.10pm								
1675.6	Ar Broadview, Sask.	6.27pm	C.T.							
	Lv Broadview	5.45pm	M.T.							
1768.4	Ar Regina	8.15pm								
	Lv Regina	11.55am		Tu	W	Th	Fr	Sa	Su	M
	Ar Saskatoon	6.05pm		W	Th	Fr	Sa	Su	M	Tu
1768.4	Lv Regina	8.15pm		Tu	W	Th	Fr	Sa	Su	M
1810.0	Ar Moose Jaw	9.20pm								
	Lv Moose Jaw	9.40pm								
1920.5	Ar Swift Current	12.30am		W	Th	Fr	Sa	Su	M	Tu
	Lv Swift Current	12.40am								
2067.9	Ar Medicine Hat, Alta.	4.30am								
	Lv Medicine Hat	4.40am								
2243.9	Ar Calgary	10.00am								
	Lv Calgary	10.05am								
	Ar Edmonton	b 5.15pm								
2325.9	Ar Banff	12.45pm								
	Lv Banff	12.55pm								
2360.5	Ar Lake Louise	2.00pm								
	Lv Lake Louise	2.05pm								
2380.4	Ar Field, B.C.	3.00pm	M.T.							
	Lv Field	2.15pm	P.T.							
2415.6	Ar Golden	a 3.35pm								
2465.5	Lv Glacier	5.25pm								
2506.3	Ar Revelstoke	7.35pm								
	Lv Revelstoke	7.45pm								
2551.1	Ar Sicamous	9.20pm								
	Lv Sicamous	9.25pm								
2635.2	Ar Kamloops	12.25am		Th	Fr	Sa	Su	M	Tu	W
	Lv Kamloops	12.35am								
2756.6	Ar North Bend	3.55am								
	Lv North Bend	4.05am								
2885.7	Ar Vancouver	9.30am								
2885.7	Lv Vancouver	10.30am								
2958.1	Ar Victoria	2.30pm	C.P. Str.							
	Lv Victoria	4.30pm								
3049.7	Ar Seattle, Wash.	8.30pm	P.T.	Th	Fr	Sa	Su	M	Tu	W

Miles	Station	Time								
0.0	Lv Seattle, Wash.	9.00am	P.T.	Su	M	Tu	W	Th	Fr	Sa
91.0	Ar Victoria, B.C.	12.45pm								
	Lv Victoria	1.45pm								
164.0	Ar Vancouver	5.45pm								
0.0	Lv Vancouver	6.30pm		Su	M	Tu	W	Th	Fr	Sa
129.1	Ar North Bend	10.15pm								
	Lv North Bend	10.25pm								
250.5	Ar Kamloops	3.00am		M	Tu	W	Th	Fr	Sa	Su
	Lv Kamloops	3.10am								
334.6	Ar Sicamous	6.10am								
	Lv Sicamous	6.15am								
379.4	Ar Revelstoke	7.45am								
	Lv Revelstoke	8.00am								
419.9	Ar Glacier	10.00am								
470.1	Lv Golden	12.00pm								
505.3	Ar Field, B.C.	1.45pm	P.T.							
	Lv Field	3.00pm	M.T.							
525.2	Ar Lake Louise, Alta.	4.15pm								
525.2	Lv Lake Louise	4.20pm								
559.9	Ar Banff	5.15pm								
	Lv Banff	5.25pm								
641.8	Ar Calgary	7.35pm								
	Lv Edmonton	a1.00pm								
	Ar Calgary	7.40pm								
817.8	Lv Calgary	7.50pm		Tu	W	Th	Fr	Sa	Su	M
	Ar Medicine Hat	12.25am								
965.2	Lv Medicine Hat	12.35am								
	Ar Swift Current, Sask.	5.00am								
	Lv Swift Current	5.10am								
1075.7	Ar Moose Jaw	8.10am								
	Lv Moose Jaw	8.20am								
1117.3	Ar Regina	9.30am								
	Lv Saskatoon	11.55pm		M	Tu	W	Th	Fr	Sa	Su
	Ar Regina	6.45am		Tu	W	Th	Fr	Sa	Su	M
1216.7	Lv Regina	9.25am		Tu	W	Th	Fr	Sa	Su	M
	Ar Broadview	12.45pm	M.T.							
	Lv Broadview	12.52pm	C.T.							
1341.0	Ar Brandon, Man.	4.00pm								
	Lv Brandon	4.10pm								
1474.1	Ar Winnipeg	7.30pm								
	Lv Winnipeg	7.50pm								
1600.0	Ar Kenora, Ont.	11.15pm								
	Lv Kenora	11.25pm								
1746.2	Ar Ignace	3.00am		W	Th	Fr	Sa	Su	M	Tu
	Lv Ignace	3.10am								
1893.4	Ar Fort William	7.00am	C.T.							
	Lv Fort William	6.15am	E.T.							
1897.8	Ar Port Arthur	8.05am								
2026.5	Lv Schreiber	12.15pm								
	Ar Schreiber	12.20pm								
2144.6	Ar White River	3.55pm								
	Lv White River	4.00pm								
2276.4	Ar Chapleau	8.00pm								
	Lv Chapleau	8.10pm								
2413.0	Ar Cartier	11.55pm								
	Lv Cartier	12.05am		Th	Fr	Sa	Su	M	Tu	W
2446.7	Ar Sudbury	1.05am								
2446.7	Lv Sudbury	1.15am								
2515.0	Ar MacTier	4.25am	No 10							
	Lv MacTier	4.35am								
2706.4	Ar Toronto (Union)	9.40am								
2446.7	Lv Sudbury	1.25am								
2525.7	Ar North Bay	3.35am								
	Lv North Bay	3.45am								
2643.4	Ar Chalk River	6.50am								
	Lv Chalk River	6.55am								
2774.4	Ar Ottawa	10.45am								
	Lv Ottawa	11.00am								
2885.7	Ar Montreal	2.00pm		Th	Fr	Sa	Su	M	Tu	W
	Ar Quebec	7.45pm								
	Ar Saint John, N.B.	11.35am		Fr	Sa	Su	M	Tu	W	Th
	Ar Portland, Me.	7.25pm								
	Ar Boston, Mass.	7.05pm								
	Ar New York, N.Y.	6.55pm	E.T.							

OPEN OBSERVATION CAR Will be placed at the rear of the Compartment Observation Car on Nos. 7 and 8 between CALGARY and REVELSTOKE

Between Montreal and Ottawa a limited number of parlor car passengers will be carried.

] PASSENGERS NOT CARRIED LOCALLY IN EITHER DIRECTION BETWEEN [
Kenora and Winnipeg. Winnipeg and Brandon. Regina and Moose Jaw. | Calgary and Sicamous. Or between Intermediate Points.

There are other Convenient Trains between these Points.

EQUIPMENT OF TRAINS Nos. 7 AND 9
- Dining Car .... Montreal to Vancouver
- Parlor Cars .... Montreal to Ottawa (2)
- Standard Sleepers .... Montreal to Vancouver (2)
  - Toronto to Vancouver (2).
  - Toronto to Sudbury.
  - Toronto to Little Current via A.E. Ry. ex. Sat. (First car July 1)
- Compartment Sleepers .... Toronto to Winnipeg.
  - Montreal to Vancouver.
- Compartment Observation ...... Montreal to Vancouver.

EQUIPMENT OF TRAINS Nos. 8 AND 10
- Dining Car .... Vancouver to Montreal and Toronto.
- Parlor Cars .... Ottawa to Montreal (2).
- Standard Sleepers .... Vancouver to Montreal (2).
  - Vancouver to Toronto (2).
  - Winnipeg to Fort William.
- Compartment Sleepers .... Winnipeg to Toronto.
  - Vancouver to Montreal.
- Compartment Observation ...... Vancouver to Montreal.

EXPLANATION OF SIGNS
E.T.—Eastern Time. C.T.—Central Time. M.T.—Mountain Time. P.T.—Pacific Time. a On Sundays leave at 7.20 a.m. b On Sundays arrive at 11.10 p.m. c Stop Westbound to entrain for Kamloops and beyond, and Eastbound to detrain from Kamloops and beyond. d On Sunday leave at 3.00 p.m. † Daily except Sunday.

*Published by kind permission of Corporate Archives, **Canadian Pacific Railway**.*

THE IMPERIAL

No. 1. WEST—Montreal to Vancouver—Daily
For detail Time Table see Tables 5 to 9

TABLE 2

No. 2. EAST—Vancouver to Montreal—Daily
For detail Time Table see Tables 5 to 9

Miles									
	Lv New York, N.Y.	8.45am	E.T	Su	M	Tu	W	Th	Fr Sa
	Lv Boston, Mass.	8.00am	"	"	"	"	"	"	"
	Lv Portland, Me.	8.10am	"	"	"	"	"	"	"
	Lv Saint John, N.B.	b 7.00pm	"	Sa	Su	M	Tu	W	Th Fr
	Lv Quebec, Que.	4.00pm	"	Su	M	Tu	W	Th	Fr Sa
0.0	Lv Montreal (C)	10.15pm	ET	Su	M	Tu	W	Th	Fr Sa
111.3	Ar Ottawa, Ont. (C)	5am	"	M	Tu	W	Th	Fr	Sa Su
	Lv Ottawa	.35	"	"	"	"	"	"	"
242.3	Ar Chalk River	6.10	"	"	"	"	"	"	"
	Lv Chalk River	6.15	"	"	"	"	"	"	"
365.0	Ar North Bay (G)	9.45	"	"	"	"	"	"	"
	Lv North Bay	10.05am	"	"	"	"	"	"	"
439.0	Ar Sudbury (C)	12.10pm	"	"	"	"	"	"	"
	Lv Sudbury	12.15	"	"	"	"	"	"	"
472.7	Ar Cartier	1.50	"	"	"	"	"	"	"
	Lv Cartier	2.00	"	"	"	"	"	"	"
609.3	Ar Chapleau	6.45	"	"	"	"	"	"	"
	Lv Chapleau	7.00	"	"	"	"	"	"	"
741.1	Ar White River	11.30	"	"	"	"	"	"	"
	Lv White River	11.40pm	"	M	Tu	W	Th	Fr	Sa Su
859.4	Ar Schreiber	4.00am	"	Tu	W	Th	Fr	Sa	Su M
	Lv Schreiber	4.15	"	"	"	"	"	"	"
987.6	Ar Port Arthur (C)	8.33	"	"	"	"	"	"	"
992.3	Ar Fort William (C)	8.50	ET	"	"	"	"	"	"
	Lv Fort William	9.10am	CT	"	"	"	"	"	"
1139.9	Ar Ignace	12.10pm	"	"	"	"	"	"	"
	Lv Ignace	12.20	"	"	"	"	"	"	"
1285.7	Ar Kenora (C)	4.25	"	"	"	"	"	"	"
	Lv Kenora	4.35	"	"	"	"	"	"	"
1411.6	Ar Winnipeg, Man. (C)	8.15	"	"	"	"	"	"	"
	Lv Winnipeg	10.30pm	"	Tu	W	Th	Fr	Sa	Su M
1544.7	Ar Brandon (U)	2.20am	"	W	Th	Fr	Sa	Su	M Tu
	Lv Brandon	2.25	"	"	"	"	"	"	"
1675.0	Ar Broadview, Sask.	6.50	CT	"	"	"	"	"	"
	Lv Broadview	9.00	MT	"	"	"	"	"	"
1768.4	Ar Regina (C)	9.35	"	"	"	"	"	"	"
	Lv Regina	9.55	"	"	"	"	"	"	"
1810.0	Ar Moose Jaw (C)	11.05	"	"	"	"	"	"	"
	Lv Moose Jaw	12.05pm	"	"	"	"	"	"	"
1920.5	Ar Swift Current (C)	2.40	"	"	"	"	"	"	"
	Lv Swift Current	2.50	"	"	"	"	"	"	"
2067.9	Ar Medicine Hat, Alta. (C)	9.25	"	W	Th	Fr	Sa	Su	M Tu
	Lv Medicine Hat	9.55pm	"	Th	Fr	Sa	Su	M	Tu W
2243.9	Ar Calgary (C)	4.15am	"	"	"	"	"	"	"
	Lv Calgary	4.30	"	"	"	"	"	"	"
2325.8	Ar Banff (C)	6.05	"	"	"	"	"	"	"
	Lv Banff	6.15	"	"	"	"	"	"	"
2360.5	v Lake Louise (C)	8.22	"	"	"	"	"	"	"
	Lv Lake Louise	6.40	"	"	"	"	"	"	"
2380.4	Ar Field, B.C.	7.45	MT	"	"	"	"	"	"
	Lv Field	10.20	PT	"	"	"	"	"	"
2415.0	Ar Golden (C)	11.50am	"	"	"	"	"	"	"
2562.5	Ar Glacier	4.25pm	"	"	"	"	"	"	"
2606.3	Ar Revelstoke (C)	4.15	"	"	"	"	"	"	"
	Lv Revelstoke	4.30	"	"	"	"	"	"	"
2551.1	Ar Sicamous	6.25	"	"	"	"	"	"	"
	Lv Sicamous	6.35	"	"	"	"	"	"	"
2635.2	Ar Kamloops (C)	9.50	"	"	"	"	"	"	"
	Lv Kamloops	10.00pm	"	Th	Fr	Sa	Su	M	Tu W
2756.6	Ar North Bend	2.55am	"	Fr	Sa	Su	M	Tu	W Th
	Lv North Bend	3.05	"	"	"	"	"	"	"
2885.7	Ar Vancouver, B.C. (C)	7.45	"	"	"	"	"	"	"
2895.7	Lv Vancouver C.P.S.tr.	10.30am	"	"	"	"	"	"	"
2960.6	Ar Victoria (D)	2.30pm	"	"	"	"	"	"	"
	Lv Victoria	4.30pm	"	"	"	"	"	"	"
3049.7	Ar Seattle, Wash.	9.30pm	PT	Fr	Sa	Su	M	Tu	W Th

OPEN OBSERVATION CAR will be placed at the rear of the Compartment Observation Car on Nos. 1 and 2 between FIELD and KAMLOOPS June 1 to September 30

Miles									
0.0	Lv Seattle, Wash. C.P.Str.	9.00am	PT	Su	M	Tu	W	Th	Fr Sa
	Lv Victoria, B.C.	12.45pm	"	"	"	"	"	"	"
81.0	Lv Victoria	1.45	"	"	"	"	"	"	"
114.0	Ar Vancouver (C)	5.45pm	"	"	"	"	"	"	"
0.0	Lv Vancouver	9.00pm	"	Su	M	Tu	W	Th	Fr Sa
129.1	Ar North Bend	1.45am	"	M	Tu	W	Th	Fr	Sa Su
	Lv North Bend	1.50	"	"	"	"	"	"	"
250.5	Ar Kamloops (C)	6.25	"	"	"	"	"	"	"
	Lv Kamloops	6.35	"	"	"	"	"	"	"
334.6	Ar Sicamous	10.30am	"	"	"	"	"	"	"
	Lv Sicamous	10.35	"	"	"	"	"	"	"
379.4	Ar Revelstoke (C)	12.25pm	"	"	"	"	"	"	"
	Lv Revelstoke	12.35	"	"	"	"	"	"	"
419.9	Ar Glacier	2.25	"	"	"	"	"	"	"
470.1	Ar Golden (C)	5.15	"	"	"	"	"	"	"
505.3	Ar Field	7.10	PT	"	"	"	"	"	"
	Lv Field	8.25	MT	"	"	"	"	"	"
525.2	Ar Lake Louise, Alta. (C)	9.35	"	"	"	"	"	"	"
	Lv Lake Louise	9.45	"	"	"	"	"	"	"
559.9	Ar Banff (C)	10.50	"	"	"	"	"	"	"
	Lv Banff	11.00pm	"	M	Tu	W	Th	Fr	Sa Su
641.8	Ar Calgary	3.00am	"	Tu	W	Th	Fr	Sa	Su M
	Lv Calgary	3.10	"	"	"	"	"	"	"
817.8	Ar Medicine Hat (C)	8.00am	"	"	"	"	"	"	"
	Lv Medicine Hat	8.10	"	"	"	"	"	"	"
965.2	Ar Swift Current, Sask. (C)	1.15pm	"	"	"	"	"	"	"
	Lv Swift Current	1.25	"	"	"	"	"	"	"
1075.7	Ar Moose Jaw (C)	5.10	"	"	"	"	"	"	"
	Lv Moose Jaw	6.05	"	"	"	"	"	"	"
1117.3	Ar Regina	7.25	"	"	"	"	"	"	"
	Lv Regina	7.35	"	"	"	"	"	"	"
1210.1	Ar Broadview	12.35am	MT	Tu	W	Th	Fr	Sa	Su M
	Lv Broadview	2.55	CT	W	Th	Fr	Sa	Su	M Tu
1341.0	Ar Brandon (C)	4.50	"	"	"	"	"	"	"
	Lv Brandon	4.55	"	"	"	"	"	"	"
1474.1	Ar Winnipeg (C)	10.00am	"	"	"	"	"	"	"
	Lv Winnipeg	1.35pm	"	"	"	"	"	"	"
1600.0	Ar Kenora, Ont. (C)	1.45	"	"	"	"	"	"	"
1746.2	Ar Ignace	5.00	"	"	"	"	"	"	"
	Lv Ignace	5.05	"	"	"	"	"	"	"
1893.4	Ar Fort William (C)	9.10	CT	"	"	"	"	"	"
	Lv Fort William	9.10	ET	"	"	"	"	"	"
1897.8	Ar Port Arthur (C)	11.25pm	"	W	Th	Fr	Sa	Su	M Tu
2026.1	Ar Schreiber	4.00am	"	Th	Fr	Sa	Su	M	Tu W
	Lv Schreiber	4.20	"	"	"	"	"	"	"
2144.6	Ar White River	8.50am	"	"	"	"	"	"	"
	Lv White River	8.55	"	"	"	"	"	"	"
2276.4	Ar Chapleau	12.55pm	"	"	"	"	"	"	"
	Lv Chapleau	1.10	"	"	"	"	"	"	"
2413.0	Ar Cartier	5.25	"	"	"	"	"	"	"
	Lv Cartier	5.45	"	"	"	"	"	"	"
2446.7	Ar Sudbury (C)	6.55pm	"	"	"	"	"	"	"
2446.7	Lv Sudbury	9.50	"	Th	Fr	Sa	Su	M	Tu W
2706.3	Ar Toronto (Union) (C)	7.00am	"	Fr	Sa	Su	M	Tu	W Th
2446.7	Lv Sudbury	7.00pm	"	Th	Fr	Sa	Su	M	Tu W
2527.7	Ar North Bay	9.15	"	"	"	"	"	"	"
	Lv North Bay	9.25	"	"	"	"	"	"	"
2643.4	Ar Chalk River	1.05am	"	Fr	Sa	Su	M	Tu	W Th
	Lv Chalk River	1.10	"	"	"	"	"	"	"
2774.4	Ar Ottawa (C)	5.10	"	"	"	"	"	"	"
	Lv Ottawa	5.30	"	"	"	"	"	"	"
2885.7	Ar Montreal, Que. (C)	8.30am	"	Fr	Sa	Su	M	Tu	W Th
	Ar Quebec	2.00pm	"	Fr	Sa	Su	M	Tu	W Th
	Ar Saint John, N.B.	c 5.10am	"	Fr	Sa	Su	M	Tu	W Th
	Ar Boston, Mass	8.00pm	"	Fr	Sa	Su	M	Tu	W Th
	Ar Portland, Me.	7.35pm	"	"	"	"	"	"	"
	Ar New York, N.Y.	9.19pm	"	Fr	Sa	Su	M	Tu	W Th

EQUIPMENT OF TRAIN No. 1
Colonist Car........Montreal—Winnipeg, Winnipeg—Vancouver.
First Class Coach..Montreal—Winnipeg, Winnipeg—Vancouver.
Tourist Sleeper....*Montreal to Vancouver.
Dining Car.........Vancouver.
Parlor Cars........Fort William to Winnipeg (Mon. & Fri.). First car May 21.
                   Banff to Kamloops (June 9-Sept. 21).
Standard Sleepers..*Montreal to Timmins (ex. Sat.) on Sat. to North Bay only.
                   *Montreal to Vancouver.
                   Fort William to Banff (Mon. & Fri.). First car May 21.
                   *Winnipeg to Moose Jaw.
                   *Winnipeg to Calgary.
                   Chicago to Vancouver (via Moose Jaw).
                   *Calgary to Vancouver.
Compartment Obs....*Montreal to Vancouver.

EQUIPMENT OF TRAIN No. 2
Colonist Car........Vancouver—Winnipeg, Winnipeg—Montreal
First Class Coach..Vancouver—Winnipeg, Winnipeg—Montreal
Tourist Sleeper....*Vancouver to Montreal.
Dining Car.........Vancouver to Montreal.
Parlor Car.........Kamloops to Banff (June 10-July 2, Sept. 5-22)
Standard Sleepers..Vancouver to Montreal.
                   Vancouver to Chicago (via Moose Jaw).
                   *Calgary to Winnipeg.
                   Moose Jaw to Winnipeg
                   eNorth Bay to Ottawa. Ready after 7.50 p.m.
Compartment Obs....Vancouver to Montreal.

*Sleepers ready for occupancy after 9.00 p.m.

EXPLANATION OF SIGNS

E.T.—Eastern Time.   C.T.—Central Time.   M.T.—Mountain Time.   P.T.—Pacific Time.
a May be occupied at Ottawa until 6.30 a.m.   b On Sundays leave at 3.00 p.m.   c On Sundays arrive at 11.35 a.m.
(C) Customs entry port for examination of baggage in bond

*Published by kind permission of Corporate Archives, **Canadian Pacific Railway**.*

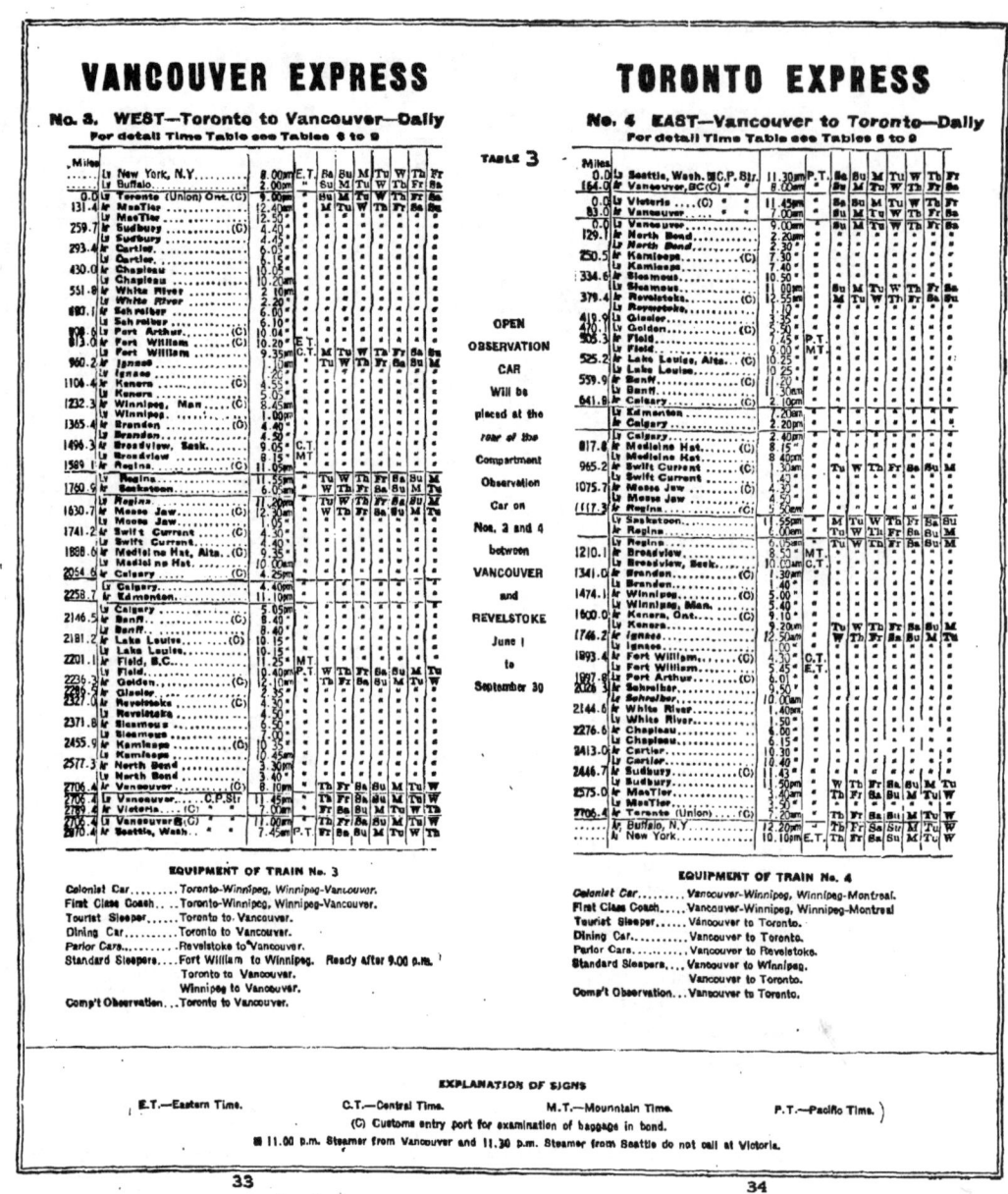

THE MOUNTAINEER
ALL-SLEEPING-CAR TRAIN

DAILY—WEST
No. 13—Chicago to Vancouver 73 00 Hrs. Mins.
(Via Soo Line and Canadian Pacific)

TABLE 4

DAILY—EAST
No. 14—Vancouver to Chicago 72 15 Hrs. Mins.
(Via Canadian Pacific and Soo Line)

Effective June 11 to September 8 from Chicago and June 15 to September 10, from Vancouver

OPEN OBSERVATION CAR Will be placed at the rear of the Compartment Observation Car on Nos. 13 and 14 between CALGARY and REVELSTOKE

Miles											Miles										
	(Grand Central Station)										0.0	Lv Seattle, Wash.	9.00am	P.T.	Su	M	Tu	W	Th	Fr	Sa
0.0	Lv Chicago, Ill.	9.45am	C.T.	Su	M	Tu	W	Th	Fr	Sa	81.0	Ar Victoria, B.C. (C)	12.45am	"	"	"	"	"	"	"	"
157.2	Lv Fond du Lac, Wis.	1.51pm	"	"	"	"	"	"	"	"	81.0	Lv Victoria	1.45"	"	"	"	"	"	"	"	"
175.0	Lv Oshkosh	2.27"	"	"	"	"	"	"	"	"	164.0	Ar Vancouver (C)	5.45"	"	"	"	"	"	"	"	"
197.0	Lv Neenah	2.51"	"	"	"	"	"	"	"	"	0.0	Lv Vancouver	7.00am	P.T.	Su	M	Tu	W	Th	Fr	Sa
250.0	Lv Stevens Point	4.45"	"	"	"	"	"	"	"	"	129.1	Ar North Bend	10.45"	"	"	"	"	"	"	"	"
449.0	Ar St. Paul, Minn.	10.25"	"	"	"	"	"	"	"	"		Lv North Bend	10.55am	"	M	Tu	W	Th	Fr	Sa	Su
	Lv St. Paul	11.00"	"	"	"	"	"	"	"	"	250.5	Ar Kamloops (C)	3.40am	"	"	"	"	"	"	"	"
460.0	Ar Minneapolis	11.30"	"	"	"	"	"	"	"	"		Lv Kamloops	3.50"	"	"	"	"	"	"	"	"
	Lv Minneapolis	11.35am									334.6	Ar Sicamous	7.03"	"	"	"	"	"	"	"	"
718.0	Lv Enderlin, N.D.	7.05am		M	Tu	W	Th	Fr	Sa	Su		Lv Sicamous	7.10"								
743	Lv Valley City	7.55"	"	"	"	"	"	"	"	"	379.4	Ar Revelstoke (C)	8.40"	"	"	"	"	"	"	"	"
813	Lv Carrington	9.45"	"	"	"	"	"	"	"	"		Lv Revelstoke	8.55"	"	"	"	"	"	"	"	"
857.0	Lv Harvey	11.00am	"	"	"	"	"	"	"	"	419.9	Ar Glacier	10.50"	"	"	"	"	"	"	"	"
930.0	Lv Minot	1.15pm	"	"	"	"	"	"	"	"		Lv Golden	12.50pm								
965.0	Lv Kenmare	2.40"	"	"	"	"	"	"	"	"	505.3	Ar Field	2.40pm								
1011.0	Ar Portal	3.35"	"	"	"	"	"	"	"	"		Lv Field	3.55"	M.T.							
1011.0	Lv North Portal, Sask. (C)	3.00"	M.T.	"	"	"	"	"	"	"	525.2	Ar Lake Louise, Alta.	5.15"	"	"	"	"	"	"	"	"
1034.0	Ar Estevan	3.50"	"	"	"	"	"	"	"	"		Lv Lake Louise (C)	5.25"	"	"	"	"	"	"	"	"
1087.0	Ar Weyburn	5.13"	"	"	"	"	"	"	"	"	559.9	Ar Banff	6.10"	"	"	"	"	"	"	"	"
1176.4	Ar Moose Jaw (C)	7.50"	"	"	"	"	"	"	"	"		Lv Banff	6.30"	"	"	"	"	"	"	"	"
	Lv Moose Jaw	8.10"	"	"	"	"	"	"	"	"	641.8	Ar Calgary	8.45"	"	"	"	"	"	"	"	"
1288.9	Ar Swift Current (C)	11.05"	"	"	"	"	"	"	"	"		Lv Calgary	9.00pm								
	Lv Swift Current	11.15"	"	"	"	"	"	"	"	"	817.8	Ar Medicine Hat (C)	1.40am	"	Tu	W	Th	Fr	Sa	Su	M
1436.1	Ar Medicine Hat, Alta. (C)	3.10am	"	Tu	W	Th	Fr	Sa	Su	M		Lv Medicine Hat	1.50"	"	"	"	"	"	"	"	"
	Lv Medicine Hat	3.20"									965.2	Ar Swift Current, Sask. (C)	6.05"	"	"	"	"	"	"	"	"
1612.3	Ar Calgary (C)	8.25"	"	"	"	"	"	"	"	"		Lv Swift Current	6.15"	"	"	"	"	"	"	"	"
1694.2	Ar Banff	11.40"									1075.7	Ar Moose Jaw (C)	9.05"	"	"	"	"	"	"	"	"
	Lv Banff	12.00n'n										Lv Moose Jaw	9.25am								
1728.9	Ar Lake Louise (C)	1.00am									1166.7	Lv Weyburn	11.50am								
	Lv Lake Louise	1.15"									1219	Lv Estevan	1.15pm								
1748.8	Lv Field, B.C.	2.00"									1243	Ar North Portal (C)	2.05am								
	Lv Field	1.15"	P.T.								1243.1	Lv Portal, N.D.	3.35am	C.T.							
	Lv Golden	2.40"									1274	Lv Kenmare	4.30"	"	"	"	"	"	"	"	"
1834.2	Ar Glacier	4.55"	"	"	"	"	"	"	"	"	1324	Lv Minot	5.55"	"	"	"	"	"	"	"	"
1874.7	Ar Revelstoke (C)	6.35"	"	"	"	"	"	"	"	"	1397	Lv Harvey	8.10"	"	"	"	"	"	"	"	"
	Lv Revelstoke	6.50"	"	"	"	"	"	"	"	"	1441	Lv Carrington	9.25"	"	"	"	"	"	"	"	"
1919.5	Ar Sicamous	8.25"	"	"	"	"	"	"	"	"	1505	Lv Valley City	11.25pm								
	Lv Sicamous	8.30"	"	"	"	"	"	"	"	"	1536	Lv Enderlin	12.05am	"	W	Th	Fr	Sa	Su	M	Tu
2003.6	Ar Kamloops (C)	11.35"	"	"	"	"	"	"	"	"	1794	Ar Minneapolis, Minn.	7.25"	"	"	"	"	"	"	"	"
	Lv Kamloops	11.45am										Lv Minneapolis	7.35"	"	"	"	"	"	"	"	"
2125.0	Ar North Bend	4.15pm									1805.1	Ar St. Paul	8.05"	"	"	"	"	"	"	"	"
	Lv North Bend	4.25"	"	"	"	"	"	"	"	"		Lv St. Paul	8.15"	"	"	"	"	"	"	"	"
2254.1	Ar Vancouver (C)	9.45pm									2004	Lv Stevens Point, Wis.	2.25pm								
2254.1	Lv Vancouver	10.30am	"	W	Th	Fr	Sa	Su	M	Tu	2057	Lv Neenah	3.57"	"	"	"	"	"	"	"	"
2337.1	Ar Victoria (C)	2.30pm									2078	Lv Oshkosh	4.13"	"	"	"	"	"	"	"	"
	Lv Victoria	4.30"									2097	Lv Fond du Lac	4.49"	"	"	"	"	"	"	"	"
2419.1	Ar Seattle, Wash.	8.30pm	"	W	Th	Fr	Sa	Su	M	Tu	2254	Ar Chicago, Ill.	9.15pm	"	"	"	"	"	"	"	"
												(Grand Central Station)									

There are other Convenient Trains between these Points. |] PASSENGERS NOT CARRIED LOCALLY IN EITHER DIRECTION BETWEEN [Calgary and Sicamous Or between Intermediate Points | There are other Convenient Trains between these Points.

EQUIPMENT OF TRAIN No. 13
Dining Car .... Chicago to Vancouver.
Standard Sleepers .... Chicago to Vancouver (2).
Chicago to Banff (2).
St. Paul to Vancouver (2).
St. Paul to Banff.
Compartment Sleeper .... Chicago to Vancouver.
Compartment Observation .... Chicago to Vancouver.

EQUIPMENT OF TRAIN No. 14
Dining Car .... Vancouver to Chicago.
Standard Sleepers .... Vancouver to Chicago (2).
Vancouver to St. Paul (2).
Banff to Chicago (2)
Banff to St. Paul.
Compartment Sleeper .... Vancouver to Chicago.
Compartment Observation .... Vancouver to Chicago.

EXPLANATION OF SIGNS

(C) Customs entry port for examination of baggage in bond.   C.T.—Central Time.   M.T.—Mountain Time.   P.T.—Pacific Time.
a Stops to detrain from Minneapolis and south, also entrain for Medicine Hat and west.
b Stops to detrain from Medicine Hat and west, also entrain for Minneapolis and south.
c Stops westbound to entrain for Kamloops and beyond, and eastbound to detrain from Kamloops and beyond.

*Published by kind permission of Corporate Archives, **Canadian Pacific Railway**.*

If Your Bookseller Does Not Yet Have This Volume:

Please Mail Orders To:
Bernard Webber
6205 – 91st Street, R.R. 1
Osoyoos, B.C., Canada, V0H 1V0

Or For More Information:
Call: (604) 495–7672

My Bank Draft or Money Order is Enclosed

for _____ Copies of "SILK TRAINS"

@ $18.95 Each (7% Canadian GST Included).

(Please Add $2.95 Shipping for Each Volume).

Please Mail To:

Name_____

Title_____

Company_____

Address_____

City_____

Prov/State_____ Code_____

Phone_____

Call Now For Special Time Limited Volume Prices!